An Allowance is Not a Bribe

An Allowance Is Not a Bribe

And other helpful hints for raising responsible ∧ children
Jewish

Allan M. Gonsher

JASON ARONSON INC.
Northvale, New Jersey
Jerusalem

This book was set in 12 pt. Bookman by Pageworks of Old Saybrook, CT and printed and bound by Book-mart Press, Inc. of North Bergen, NJ.

Library of Congress Cataloging-in-Publication Data

Gonsher, Allan.
    An allowance is not a bribe : and other helpful hints for raising responsible Jewish children / by Allan Gonsher.
        p.   cm.
    Includes bibliographical references and index.
    ISBN 0–7657–6133–5
    1. Child rearing—Religious aspects—Judaism.
2. Parenting—Religious aspects—Judaism.   3. Jewish families—
Religious life.   4. Jewish religious education of children.
5. Parenting—Psychological aspects. I. Title.

HQ769.3.G66 2000
649'.157924—dc21   99–052081

Printed in the United States of America on acid-free paper. For information and catalog write to Jason Aronson Inc., 230 Livingston Street, Northvale, NJ 07647–1726, or visit our website: www.aronson.com.

To my partner and best friend, Rini, and to our inspirations Josh, Ben, and Zack

Contents

Contents

Foreword: The Jewish Journey

PARENTING JEWISHLY

This book about raising Jewish children is different from any of the parenting books currently in print. In this book I call upon my working knowledge of psychology and family dynamics to make a case for effective parenting as the basis for children's emotional health, and I single out consistent, loving discipline as the key to effective parenting. I address a broad range of situations that Jewish parents encounter in raising their children, demonstrate ways to prevent problems, and suggest solutions to difficulties once they've occurred. The eyes, heart, and mind of a Jewish therapist come to bear in all the advice I offer. Frequently I combine proven discipline techniques with Jewish traditions, beliefs, and practices.

This book isn't another "how to" on such matters as observing Jewish holidays or keeping a Kosher home—as are books previously written by teachers and scholars—nor another discussion of overall parenting skills, sprinkled with a few particularly "Jewish issues," as you might find in existing books by psychologists or others. Rather, in these chapters I demonstrate how a Torah-based life has answered the deepest personal needs within me and the members of my family and has provided my wife and me the tools for effective parenting.

What qualifies me? I'm a family and children's therapist with more than twenty-five years in the counseling field; I'm also a husband of twenty-eight years and the father of three grown sons. In my counseling practice, I help parents and children communicate, express their deepest feelings, resolve differences, and restore harmony to their lives. I introduce parents and children to the coping skills they need to meet life's challenges, come to terms with disappointments, and achieve their fullest potential. I often use the wisdom found in Judaism to guide my clients.

Who is my audience? I expect that many of my readers would define themselves as members of one or another Jewish group—Orthodox, Conservative, or Reform. To me, a more significant categorization would be along these lines: first, parents whose Jewish customs and religious practices are already meaningful and satisfying to them . . . or second, parents seeking the ways and means to increase the Jewishness in their homes and lives. Do you see yourself in either profile? If so, I sincerely hope you will find reassurance, guidance, and points of interest in this book. Much of what I've presented here comes from my strong belief in traditional Jewish ritual as a framework and guide for life. I recognize that a reader here or there might accuse me of depending too much on traditional ritual in the face of today's complex family issues. I respond, "Precisely!" The strength of this book comes from my reliance on God and my trust in the worth of carrying out His commandments. This is not coincidental. I'm a serious Jew committed to following the principles of the Torah. To reach what I've become, I've traveled a long path filled with difficult questions, inner struggles, and partial resolutions. I call this path my "Jewish Journey." Because I've made the journey, I'm prepared to help parents get started on theirs, and to advise and support others as they proceed on their way. You'll see such guidance throughout every chapter.

Prior to the chapters themselves, you'll notice a second part to this foreword. It's subtitled "Your Jewish Journey," and it's meant especially for parents considering ways to increase the Jewish dimension in their life. If you *are* one such parent, I want you to know you're among an increasing number. In my practice, and in my personal life, I come in contact again and again with parents who have a strong desire to create a more faith-based, ritual-motivated lifestyle, but aren't sure exactly how to go about it. This book talks about the yearnings, uncertainties, potential pitfalls, and ultimate rewards associated with taking the Jewish Journey.

Let me say this to every one of my readers: Whether you have toddlers or teenagers, whether your Jewishness is defined or in progress—whatever point you've reached on your personal Jewish Journey—I passionately hope this book will make a contribution to your role as a Jewish parent.

YOUR JEWISH JOURNEY

It's probably needless to say that any person moving toward a more Jewish lifestyle may encounter obstacles. I will assure you, however, that the results are ultimately worth it, in terms of personal fulfillment as well as parental effectiveness.

Of course, the process tends to be easier if you and your spouse, together, make the decision for a family change. Even so, it is not unrealistic to expect some degree of turmoil with your children, extended family, and friends. They might be uncomfortable with your decision to "become more Jewish"; they might seem unwilling to accept the changes they observe in your life; they might challenge your motives; they might even call you a "fanatic" and/or disassociate themselves from you. If you undergo painful experiences such as these, you'll have to take a step back and reconsider your developing commitment. You'll need to ask yourself, again, "Who am I? What am I? What does Jewishness mean to me? How much does it mean to me to have Jewish children and grandchildren?"

Let me offer a few words of encouragement. I think your personal belief and passion will be two of the most important supports along your way.

You need to believe in yourself and your children to proceed successfully. Do all you can to include friends and family in your journey; expect some setbacks; when the going gets rough, try not to become too discouraged. Remember, you are not alone.

Chazack, chazack, venetchazek. Be strong, be strong, and we will be strengthened. I can assure you, from my own experience, that your perseverance will be well worth the effort.

In closing this foreword, I'd like to express my gratitude to the following individuals: Ellen Gordman, for putting my thoughts and words into readable form; Diane Axler Baum, for polishing every sentence with love; my wife, Rini, for her support and her deep interest in my work; and my sons, Josh, Ben, and Zack, for inspiring me to continue working with and enjoying children. I also want to express my appreciation to my Mom and Dad who gave me what I needed to succeed in life, and my thanks to God who gives my life its meaning. Finally, this book is dedicated to you, and to all parents who are working every day to be the best possible moms and dads they can be.

PART ONE

Chapter 1
Parenting 101

Much of the information in this book is based on my own experience as a children's therapist and father of three sons. As I undertook the task of parenting, I was fortunate that my wife and I shared the same aspirations for our children. Both Rini and I wanted our children to appreciate each day, to develop a connection with the Eternal God, to be in awe of the spiritual breadth of the universe. We wanted their lives to have meaning, purpose, and direction through *mitzvot* (commandments), and we were committed to having a strong Jewish home enriched by the beliefs and rituals of our faith. We were equally determined to practice loving, firm, consistent discipline as the keystone for childrearing. Looking back over the past twenty-plus years, we're gratified that we made the right choices and enjoyed more than a little *mazel.* Today, our eldest son, Joshua, having returned from study in Israel, attends a college and yeshiva in New York. Our middle son, Benjamin, is studying in Israel, as is our youngest, Zachary.

Don't think the years have been problem-free! Rini and I confronted challenges daily, and I know we are no different from other parents. What really counts is the result, and for Rini and me, it was what we were working toward. We have managed to raise three responsible, Jewish sons.

You, also, have what it takes to raise responsible, Jewish sons and daughters. This book is intended to guide you on the way. First and foremost, I hope this book will inspire you to think seriously about your own Jewish Journey as the basis for your personal fulfillment and for being the best parents you can be. To prepare you for the individual chapters, let's take a few moments here to discuss my particular overview of the Jewish parenting picture. This is my "Parenting 101," which looks at a number of issues: spousal agreement; inter-personal communication; internal and external tranquility; parental expectations; parental role-modeling; and, of the utmost importance, the ways and the means of bringing God into your kids' lives . . . and keeping Him there.

PARENTS, CHILDREN, AND GOD

In my work with families and in my personal life, I have observed that young children embrace the concept of God's existence. At approximately four to six years of age, children ask questions about sex, birth, death, and God. At this early stage, they are willing and able to accept their parents' explanations regarding spirituality, faith, and the relationship between the Divine Being and human beings. They are willing—in fact, I have seen them demonstrate a need—to develop a relationship with God and to carry out rituals, such as the saying of prayers. For children, it's a natural and normal part of the developmental process. It's as natural and normal a stage of development as the progression from parallel play to group play, or becoming ready to share toys, or cooperate, or follow directions. What does this mean for Jewish parents? It means that Jewish parents need to acknowledge, appreciate, and grasp this stage in their children's lives to foster spirituality, a connection to God, and a love of Jewish ritual. The ability of parents to assist their children in negotiating this normal, developmental stage depends largely on how much they understand their inner selves and their own reactions to issues of faith, spirituality, and ritual. In other words, if parents project their own "hang-ups" onto their kids, they hinder them from fully understanding and appreciating their true feelings. (Whose problem is it, anyway?) I suggest taking a few small steps at a time. Start when your kids are about three. Show them how to light *Shabbat* candles, and they'll look forward to lighting them every week. Sing Chanukah songs, and they'll sing them with you. Teach them prayers, like the *Shema* before bed, and they'll easily get into a routine of saying their prayers again and again. Ask them to wash their hands before saying a blessing over bread, and they'll gladly do it. It's no different from teaching them to respect their teachers, brush their teeth morning and night, operate the water faucets for their daily shower, or behave politely at the dinner table. Setting standards and making expectations are the parents' right and responsibility. It would make sense that you should view your child's spiritual development as one of the many aspects of growing up that require you to show the way.

Preteens Will Challenge

Even for the most diligent parents, however, their kids' preteen years bring new demands. Often, at age eleven or twelve, children begin to challenge every value that parents have tried so hard to instill, including matters of religion and faith. Your preteens are apt to question and doubt; they may proclaim themselves to be agnostics, humanists, atheists. How sad that many Jewish children at approximately age thirteen are very likely to undergo a rite of passage which is diametrically opposed to the Judaism their parents have been teaching them! Ironically, just as they complete the Bar or Bat Mitzvah—with its expectation of enforcing and reinforcing their Jewish commitment—they may, instead, proceed to a stage that I call the "atheistic struggle," characterized by a rejection of faith, religion, and belief in God. If they are left on their own at this stage, I foresee three possible outcomes. Most unfortunate is the inclination to cut themselves off from their Judaism and never return. Let's face it, if their rejection of faith, religion, and God is not reversed by the time they reach their early twenties, chances are they'll date non-Jews, put their early Judaism behind them, select a non-Jewish spouse, and raise non-Jewish children. Of course, another possibility exists. They may find a Jewish partner with whom they will begin, again, to develop a Jewish identity. Just say the latter occurs. Then what do you have? You have a young man or woman whose spiritual faith was arrested at around age twelve or thirteen. If, upon becoming a parent, this individual decides to raise children within the Jewish faith (as surely we would hope and pray!), I see a real problem. How, I ask, will a person who has reached only a preteen level of spirituality have the ability to convey, with passion and conviction, a deep and meaningful commitment to Judaism? How can this individual help but pass on pessimism, skepticism, lack of knowledge, and defensiveness? In other words, I see the threat of "Pediatric Judaism" attempting to be "Mature Judaism." Surely this is not what we Jews should mean by "generation to generation," *L'dor v'dor*!

This is why I firmly believe we parents need to be honest with ourselves as we struggle with matters relating to Jewish values, Jewish belief, Jewish practices, and God. Notice, I said "struggle with," not "resolve." It's truly okay if you haven't reached your final conclusions. What's imperative, however, is that you start thinking. Don't get "hung up" if you haven't solidified every aspect of your belief structure; but do get "hung up" if you are a parent and you haven't started the process. Why? Because, your job as a parent is to raise emotionally healthy children; and any Jewish parent who has not started thinking about Jewishness and

God is failing to fulfill even the very first require-
ment. Moreover, you owe it to yourself. I promise
you that starting your Jewish Journey will launch
you on the most valuable life adventure you will
ever undertake. If we're willing (and we are!) to
struggle with the issues of the secular world, then
we must be willing to take the same amount of
time and energy to struggle with matters that relate
to our souls and spirituality.

I know I'm hitting you with difficult concepts.
Most of us would prefer to spare ourselves the
work, the agony, of wrestling with tough ideas. But
it must be done. You're willing to think long and
hard about how to finance your new home, about
gymnastics classes versus singing lessons for your
eight-year-old daughter, about your ten-year-old
son's readiness for overnight camp, and countless other secular issues. From the time your
children are quite young, you must prepare yourself to work equally hard on spiritual and religious
issues.

A Jewish parent's efforts in these areas continue over many long years. As your kids reach
their early teens, seize every opportunity to help
them relate to other human beings and to God.
Remember to make time to acknowledge and discuss with your kids the relationship that exists
between their souls and their bodies. Talk to them

about the spiritual and the physical. Such discussions are as vital as open communication about sexuality, alcohol, and drugs. Be available to your kids every step of their way, so they'll never be alone in struggling with the many issues that confront them, including spirituality, Jewish identity, and God. During some points in your children's development, you may need to work even harder at being good Jewish role models. You may have to strengthen the structure that promotes Judaism in your home, and more diligently encourage your kids to continue their involvement in Jewish activities. How you handle these kinds of situations will depend on your own developing Jewish identity as you proceed on your personal Jewish Journey.

I remember that Rini and I were especially careful when our boys reached their preteen and teenage years. Sure, at home we continued to celebrate the holidays and festivals and to observe *Shabbat*. In addition, we made plans for our boys to leave Omaha regularly to be with other committed Jewish youth to share Jewish experiences such as camps and conclaves. We encouraged study of Jewish sources with the support and in the company of Jewish mentors.

As you proceed on your personal Jewish Journey, and as your children develop and grow, you may continue to confront inner struggles. Still, I urge you to start the process and to continue to give it major attention. Perhaps you'll begin by thinking seriously about issues of faith; then, you'll move on to the regular performance of one or two or three *mitzvot*; and then you'll proceed in the direction of placing higher and higher priority on performing increasing numbers of *mitzvot*. I sincerely hope that wrestling with the difficult concepts of faith and belief will lead you to accept the existence of God and the need to carry out His commandments. I'm convinced that such an acknowledgment will empower you to gain the full benefit of your Judaism and of life itself. I'm equally convinced, however, of a corollary that also comes from my observations. I believe that Jewish parents and their children can benefit by "believing some and practicing some." What truly counts is that parents accept the process and the need to continually address the issues.

At this point, I will make an assumption: I've persuaded you to think seriously about all that you've just read. Whatever you decide, or while you decide, I invite you to continue reading. Let's push on with the "Parenting 101" as promised at the beginning of this chapter.

AGREEMENT AND DISAGREEMENT

You and your spouse won't always agree. Each spouse comes into the parenting picture with an individual background. Each of you has different beliefs, feelings, aspirations, and reactions to life and living—including your Judaism. Therefore it's very likely you will disagree on any number of specific issues, such as bedtime, allowance, homework, chores, synagogue attendance, *Shabbat* observance, or missing Hebrew School to play in the soccer game. Even so, you can raise your children in a firm and consistent environment which emphasizes responsibility and respect. You can work together toward compromises that meet children's and parents' needs. When you and your spouse disagree but come to an accommodation, your children learn that differences of opinion are okay. Hopefully, they also will learn a few communication skills! If you and your spouse disagree on many issues, successful discipline will be more difficult, but still not impossible to accomplish.

I believe that *Shalom Bayit* (domestic tranquility) depends first on open communication between husband and wife, and second on clearly delineated responsibilities.[1] Couples should decide which household jobs will be cooperative, husband-wife efforts; which jobs will be handled predominantly by the wife; and which will be handled predominantly by the husband. (Who will take primary responsibility for balancing the checkbook, corresponding with out-of-town relatives, winterizing the cars, planting the flower garden, driving the children to Hebrew school, building the sukkah, preparing the home for Passover . . . .)

I'm not referring to "woman's work" and "man's work." I'm a firm believer that husbands should help in the kitchen and wives, in the yard. I'm suggesting that each spouse should be responsible for specific tasks, and that each should be flexible, cooperative, and willing to help the other. There's a corollary here: Each spouse must remember the importance of communicating with the other when help, support, and cooperation are needed.

The importance of cooperation and communication applies as well to the parent–child relationship. Boys and girls should be expected to help their parents in all areas of running the household, such as laundry, meal preparation, raking leaves, welcoming guests, etc. That way, children will learn a variety of skills, and they will come to appreciate different kinds of work. Moreover, parents will have opportunities to be with their children in different settings. They will become accustomed to responding effectively to a range of children's behaviors and to meting out discipline when necessary.

Many Jewish practices serve, at once, to provide harmony in the home and to set the stage for more. *Shabbat* observance stands out as the most obvious example. It's also a good example of my confidence in traditional ritual as a remedy for today's complex family issues. In our too-busy society, where parents and kids might not see each other from one day to the next, isn't it wonderful to share one night each week—not only being together, but all focused on the same thing. Think, for a moment, about the dynamics. Children are expected to clean up their rooms and bathe and dress for the occasion. They're encouraged to set the holiday table, gather the *kipot* (skull caps) and candles, and help their mother prepare the food. The very act of kindling *Shabbat* candles holds the potential for a powerful, positive effect on each person present. Husband, wife, and children have delineated roles. 1) The wife traditionally lights the candles, bringing a glow of warmth into the home; 2) the husband further emphasizes the sanctity of the occasion by reciting the Kiddush (ceremonial blessing); and 3) the children welcome the beauty of the Sabbath as they chant the *Shalom Aleichem* (the Jewish song welcoming the

Sabbath). On yet a deeper level, each member of the family takes "time out" to share the past week's experiences, and communicate meaningfully with one another.

PARENTS ARE ROLE MODELS

Children will imitate your behaviors, both good and bad. You can be a positive role model by giving regularly to charity, attending synagogue services, relating with kindness and understanding to your spouse, and expressing your feelings openly. Remember, your children are more likely to respond to your actions than your words. So, it's important for *you* to do what you want *them* to do.

Children will learn positive behavior from Jewish role models who are good, stable, honest, and sincere. Conversely, they will learn negative behavior from dishonest or insincere role models. For example, you ask for time off from work to observe Rosh Hashanah. You go to services in the morning, but you leave early to attend a ball game. Your actions say two negative things to your children. It's okay to tell your employer (or teacher) half truths; and it's okay to treat your religious commitments less than wholeheartedly.

Role-modeling comes to bear in teaching your

children the significance of Jewish customs and practices. You show your children the relevance of Judaism in your life and in theirs when you go to the synagogue, observe holidays, say blessings, pray, keep kosher, visit the sick, provide meals for the elderly, and follow other rituals. If, however, you ignore basic customs and traditions, you communicate to your children that you don't consider them very important.

I can't think of a better way to promote togetherness than by celebrating Jewishly. In my family, just to provide one example, the holiday of Sukkot made every autumn special. After building and decorating the sukkah together, we all invited friends to share as many meals as possible within it. Rini and I have wonderful memories of these times together. Even more important, our sons have expressed a desire to carry on our traditions when they have families of their own.

Strive for "Inner Tranquility"

You must parent with love, not anger. Maimonides discusses the role of anger in one's personality.[2] He considers anger negative and harmful, and he believes that Jews are responsible for controlling it. His teachings tell us that parents should strive for internal calm and at least the reduction, if not the total elimination, of anger. He believes that parents, even at the most stressful moment, should attempt to replace feelings of rage with love and kindness. He speaks of working toward what he calls "inner tranquility."

It takes tremendous determination to achieve such a level of self-control. It's almost a matter of expunging anger and angry feelings from your soul. How should you go about it? Allow yourself to express anger only for the purpose of convincing your kids of the seriousness of the infraction. Never permit your anger to become a verbal weapon that undermines, belittles, or demeans your children.

Rini and I are friendly with a couple who have eight kids. One Friday night our family was invited to share *Shabbat* dinner with them. When we arrived, we sensed an atmosphere of chaos. While the wife was finishing final dinner preparations, several children were still getting dressed, and more than one sibling fight had ensued. I expected the father to be in a frenzy as he tried to bring about order. Instead, he took one step at a time. He calmly separated the children who were fighting; he directed the older boys and girls to assist their mother; he set about helping the younger children put on their *Shabbat* clothing. Soon, we all sat down to a delightful meal with all the children participating and having a good time. This father is an excellent example of how a parent's internal calm and self-confidence can be used to create a loving environment to which children respond positively.

GIVE UNDIVIDED ATTENTION

Spend "soft moments" with your kids. "Soft moments" are those times when you give a child your undivided attention and really listen to what is being said to you. These encounters can occur when you're riding in the car together, preparing for bed, eating a meal, studying Torah, or shooting baskets in your driveway. If you don't interrupt, lecture, analyze, or evaluate, your son or daughter will most likely use this opportunity to tell you what's actually going on in his or her life. During such moments when you ask, "What's up?" your child is likely to open up to you. You should work hard at developing as many of these opportunities as possible when your kids are younger. If you do, you will have less trouble creating them when your kids become preteens or teenagers. Even if they already are teenagers, it's not impossible to start, just a bit more difficult.

When my sons were younger, I started the practice of spending one-on-one time alone with each of them weekly. Sometimes we had a special outing, like going to a movie; sometimes we simply stopped for a quick breakfast together on the way to school. I'd let them do the talking as I listened carefully without interrupting, criticizing, or judging. Today, as my sons reach their mature identities—especially their mature Jewishness—they talk with me about the challenges and struggles they face and the resolutions they reach. The lines of communication are open, and they freely share their thoughts and feelings with me. They discuss with me such issues as their behavior with girls, drinking, keeping curfew, studying Torah, and following the commandments. If you are the parent of a young adult, you can appreciate why this gives me a tremendous feeling of gratitude and accomplishment!

Maintain a Sense of Humor

Being a parent is one of the most difficult jobs you'll ever undertake. Sometimes you'll feel you've gone three steps backward for every single step forward. Consistent effort, plenty of *mazel* (luck), and God's help are necessary to become good parents. However, there can be fun and joy in a house with growing, active children. Through your children you can relive the delightful times of your own childhood, such as swimming on a hot afternoon, seeing a favorite movie again, going to a Purim carnival, marching around the synagogue on Simchat Torah, or looking at old family photos. You'll have wonderful memories of these times together.

Listen carefully to your children, because as Art Linkletter so correctly noted, "Kids say the darnedest things." Even though my sons are young adults now, I remember some of their truly funny statements. Speaking from my own experience, I believe that the enjoyable times outnumber the frustrating ones. I wish the same for you.

Know What's Appropriate

To be effective at disciplining your children, you need to know what is normal and appropriate behavior and what is normal, but not appropriate, for each developmental stage. The Mishnah explains that children are ready at different ages to learn specific tasks.[3] This reference tells parents that they need to be mindful of each child's developmental capabilities. Once parents accept this concept, they can extend its meaning by encouraging behavior that's appropriate, and discouraging conduct that isn't.

Many actions may be normal for a child's age but not acceptable. For example, a two-year-old may bite another child to alleviate feelings of frustration or anger, but this behavior shouldn't be allowed to continue. It may be normal for teenagers to try smoking or drinking, but as these behaviors are illegal, they must be stopped. Your children might take the money earmarked for the *tzedakah* box (charity or alms box) and spend it on candy, skip afternoon Hebrew School to play with friends, or eat *treife* (non-Kosher foods). If they do, you must respond accordingly. A violation of "Jewish behavior" must be on at least the same level as a violation of "secular behavior."

You should establish rules and limits according to each child's age and communicate your expectations for good behavior. You also need to tell your children what the consequences will be for breaking rules or exceeding the limits. You must be firm and consistent in maintaining limits and disciplining infractions.

RELATIONSHIPS BEYOND THE HOME

Relationships outside the family are important for children. The Mishnah teaches that you must "accept upon yourself a teacher and acquire a friend."[4] These two persons will be instrumental in matters of studying and learning from Torah, imparting religious beliefs and practices, and learning how to deal with life's challenges. You don't have the time or the skills to help your children develop every aspect of their lives. There are other people—such as teachers, coaches, scout leaders, and relatives—who will have a positive impact on your children. You need to assure that your children have opportunities to spend time with numerous individuals who can help them grow into responsible adults.

Another synagogue's youth group had an advisor whom Rini and I liked very much because he followed all of the Jewish beliefs and values we were trying to instill in our sons. We made sure our boys spent additional time with him outside of youth group activities. We invited him to our house for *Shabbat* dinners, holiday celebrations, and other family activities. The boys liked this young man and enjoyed spending time with him. On several occasions he helped us resolve con-

flicts with the boys, because they respected him
and were willing to listen to his advice.

HONOR THY PARENTS

The Torah says "Honor your father and your
mother, so that your days will be lengthened upon
the land that *Hashem*, your God, gives you."[5]
Children should be taught from an early age that
one of the greatest *mitzvot* (commandments) they
can perform is to honor their parents.[6] Here are
a few of the countless examples of Jewish teaching on the subject: Isaac's father, Abraham, asked
him to climb upon the altar to be sacrificed, and
Isaac obeyed without questioning.[7] The Talmud
makes many references to honoring parents, such
as in the story of Rav Tarfon, who provided his
body as a step stool for his mother to help her get
in and out of bed.[8] Honoring takes the form of
serving in the *Sefer Hamitzvot*, Positive Commandment 41, which mandates that we provide our
parents with food, drink, and clothing.

What does this mean in practical, everyday
terms? Children must show respect for their parents even when they disagree with them. At times
your children will think your standards of behav-

ior and the discipline you impart are too strict; they will be resentful. Even so, they *must* respect you as the ultimate authority. Do I hear you scoffing under your breath? Was that "Yeh, right" I heard from you? I understand your reaction. That's exactly why I wrote this book. I can assure you without a doubt, parents can gain control of their kids if they exercise firm, consistent authority in an environment of kindness and mutual respect. You can do it. You must.

While my sons were growing up, if they exhibited any disrespectful behavior, they had to spend time alone in their rooms. If they failed to complete school work properly and their grades suffered, they were grounded. If they were noisy during synagogue services, they lost privileges. Rini and I allowed them to express their feelings in a calm and courteous manner. We didn't change our minds about the debated issues, but we established a relationship of mutual respect. By being firm, consistent, and committed to one approach, we convinced them that we meant business. I know this task is far from easy, but I also know that you can do it if you are firm and consistent.

From experience, I know that if kids are allowed to be discourteous and disrespectful, they're at risk for developing disastrous traits. Their lack of self control will make problems for them in relating to authority figures such as teachers, coaches, and principals and later to bosses in the workplace. It's up to parents to "set their kids straight" as early as possible and keep them that way.

Things to Consider

- Remember this is the most difficult task we have undertaken.
- Involve God and commandments in your life.
- Conflict is part of the process of parenting. Work hard at resolution.
- Parents' "Jewish Journey" will have a dramatic impact on children's "Jewish Journey." Be intellectually honest while addressing this adventure.
- Distinguish between appropriate and normal.
- Raising children requires a cooperative effort between family, friends, community, and God.

Endnotes

1. Talmud, *Bava Metziah* 59a, discusses this "job exclusivity."

2. Mishna Torah, *Hilchot Dayot* (The Laws of Knowledge) 2:3.
3. Mishnah, *Pirkei Avot* (Ethics of the Fathers) 5:25.
4. Ibid. 1:6.
5. Torah, *Exodus* 20:12.
6. The mitzvah to honor one's parents is one of only three *mitzvot* where the Torah indicates its reward for the observance. The others are leaving the baby bird in the nest (*Deuteronomy* 22:6–7) and taking the sabbatical year (*Leviticus* 25:20).
7. Torah, *Genesis* 22:9.
8. Talmud, *Kiddushin* 31b.

Chapter 2
An Allowance Is Not a Bribe

Allowance. The word is enough to make kids whoop with glee and send parents into a panic mode. Children expect to receive an allowance. Parents, although they know children need money, often are confused about the issue of money in their children's lives. At what age should children begin to receive their own spending money? How much should they get? What expenses should they be expected to cover on their own?

Money can serve as a positive or negative force. We all know people who have allowed money to control their lives or have misused it for destructive purposes. We know other people who use their money wisely, to benefit themselves and also to help those less fortunate.

The Vilna Gaon, an eighteenth-century rabbi, differentiated three uses of money—for *mitzvot* such as acts of loving kindness; for the necessities of life; and for saving in anticipation of expenses.[1] Recognizing the importance of money in the world, it's obvious that parents must teach their kids how to manage their money so that it doesn't end up managing them. What a benefit it is to children to learn, through allowance, how to be financially responsible.

I believe there's only one way to give an allowance to children. It's what I call the "I Love You Allowance." Children get an allowance not because they're good or bad, not because they've done their chores, but simply because their parents love them. The allowance is not a reward for chores well done and isn't withheld as punishment.

When you give your kids an allowance without any strings attached, you're saying, "I love you unconditionally." This isn't to say that money is an object of love. An unconditional allowance—an act of pure giving—sends the message that your love isn't dependent on any particular action or response by your child.

Why is it so important to separate allowance from behavior? I have found that it seldom works to connect an allowance to conduct or to the performance of chores. You may tell your daughter she has to do five chores each week to get her $3 allowance. If she only does two chores, does she get $1.70? If she does four chores, does she get $2.40? The reward allowance can lead to negotiating and fighting between parents and children.

DOING THEIR SHARE

Your children should have a list of chores they need to do simply because they live in the house. When my boys cleaned their rooms for *Shabbat* or set the table for a *Yom Tov* (holiday) meal, they were thanked for their efforts, not paid. They received their set allowance whether they did their chores, behaved at school, or attended junior congregation on Saturday mornings. If they misbehaved or failed to complete assigned chores, they received an appropriate punishment, such as going to bed early or spending time in their room. You may want to consider preparing a list of chores your children can do to earn extra money. For example, you would pay them $2 to rake leaves in the yard; $15 to vacuum, wipe down, and rearrange the closets at the change of a season; $10 to clean the kitchen cupboards for Passover; $5 to help set up the sukkah. This list should be posted on the refrigerator where it's readily available for your children to see and choose from.

It's up to you to determine how much allowance to give your kids and whether part of the money goes into a savings account. It will be difficult to watch them waste their money playing video games or buying candy. You might be tempted to "micro-manage" your children's money so they don't waste it. Remember that one purpose of an allowance is to teach financial responsibility. This can be accomplished only if a child is given the freedom to spend some money without your guidance and has the leeway to make mistakes and learn from them. Who controls the savings account? Before a savings account is set up, determine whether you or your child controls it. If you don't take this precaution, there will be fights over how savings are spent. Parents should control the savings account of a child under five. For older kids there are other options. Decisions about spending the savings can be made by parents and children jointly, by parents alone, or by children alone.

When our boys were growing up, they often wanted to buy Jewish items such as a book, *tzitzit* (prayer shawl for kids), a *yarmulke* (skull cap), or a *mezuzah* (small piece of parchment inscribed with *Deuteronomy* 6:4-9). Rini and I never restricted these kinds of purchases. But we did limit their buying of fad items such as posters, CDs, and computer games.

Spending or Saving

An allowance works as a great tool for learning how to spend money wisely and learning what it means to save for a special purpose. Suppose your son has put his nickels and dimes away each week and has saved $50. Then he takes the money and buys the shoddiest toy ever made which breaks within a week. This will be painful for you to observe, but your child will learn from this experience how to be more selective when spending his precious money. As my boys matured, they wanted to visit friends they had made at *Shabbatonim* or summer camps. They had to save their own money to pay for such trips. From experience they learned that if they spent money on video games or going out with their friends, it took longer to save for a plane ticket. They also discovered they could accumulate money faster if they did the extra chores posted on the refrigerator.

An allowance helps kids learn how to make choices. For example, you and your daughter go shopping at the mall, and she asks you to buy her a new doll. You suggest she use her allowance, or a portion of it, to buy the doll. She must choose between the instant gratification of buying the doll now, or the delayed reward of saving for that new bike she's wanted.

Parents wonder how much money they should give their children. There is no standard amount for allowances. Our boys started receiving an allowance of 50 cents each week upon turning five. In the following years, the amount increased, up to $3. With this money the boys were expected to take responsibility for certain types of purchases.

Regardless of the size of the allowance, you need to decide what will work best for each of your kids. You might give your older children a larger amount of money and expect them to pay for their school lunches, their own clothes, and entertainment. Or you might pay for major expenses and give your children a nominal amount of money to spend for incidentals like gum, candy, and comic books. The older the child, the greater the allowance should be. Periodic increases in the allowance can be negotiated, but parents must maintain the final say. (In other words, don't let your children dictate the terms!) As your children get older, you want to encourage them to seek other sources of income, rather than remain dependent upon you for all their money.

Kids need to learn at an early age to help those who are less fortunate. Teach your children to save part of their allowance for *tzedakah* (charity). Although you may have a *pushke* (charity box) in your home, consider giving your children their own. Putting money in the *pushke* is very impersonal, so you should also encourage hands-on giving. Children can do something as simple as buying a can of food to put in the food bank cart at the grocery store or giving to the Jewish Free Loan Society or to Jewish Family Services for holiday distribution programs. If a *meshulach* (collector) comes to the door, involve your children in making him feel at home and giving him money.

The "I Love You Allowance" has the potential to avoid fights and help your children learn how to handle their money. It will also teach your children about unconditional love and about financial responsibility.

THINGS TO CONSIDER

- Teach by example. Show your children how you manage the family finances, including saving for future expenses such as car insurance, college tuition, or a trip to Israel.

- Help your children invest their money so they see financial rewards in delaying gratification.
- Don't use money as a bribe to change your children's behaviors.
- Don't bail your children out after they've made bad financial decisions.
- Make *tzedakah* a priority in your kids' lives.

ENDNOTE

1. *Commentary to Proverbs* 13:4.

Chapter 3
No, Because I Said So

When I was growing up, I hated it when my parents said, "No, because I said so." I decided that when I had kids, I'd never, ever say those words to them. Well, I became wiser when I had children of my own. I discovered that being an effective parent sometimes requires the proclamation, "No, because I said so."

Parents shouldn't be afraid to say, "Do it, because I told you to" in a kind and loving manner. Children's self-esteem will not be damaged if they aren't given fifty reasons why they must follow your directions. True, they might resent you and be angry with you for the moment, but that's better than ending up with children who can't control their behavior.

The Torah offers many examples of how God commanded an individual to take a specific action without giving a reason or explanation. He expected the individual to fully follow his instructions. In the Torah, God said to Abraham, "Please take your son, your only one, whom you love, Yitzchak (Isaac), and go to the land of Moriah; bring him up there as an offering. . . ."[1] God gave no reason to Abraham for doing what was asked. The message was, "Do this because I told you to." Abraham obeyed without question and benefited greatly by becoming the father of our people.

In other instances, God offered more information when making specific demands. For example, in reference to the apple, God said to Eve, "You shall neither eat of it nor touch it, lest you die."[2] God explained to Eve what the results would be if she engaged in a specific behavior, eating the fruit from the tree of knowledge. Despite the warning, Eve disobeyed God, and she and Adam were expelled from the Garden of Eden. This shows the negative impact on a person's life that can result from challenging authority.

You are entitled to make demands of your children without giving any reasons, just as God did to Abraham, or without lengthy explanations, as in the case of Eve. In fact, in the Torah an overwhelming number of *mitzvot* (commandments) are unexplained.

When you give your children too many reasons why they should go to bed at a certain time or eat their vegetables or go to Sunday School, you lose control. You may think your children will respond to a long list of rational reasons, but it usually doesn't work that way. Children will begin to argue and challenge the reasons, and then the whole encounter will turn into a shouting match.

However, if you focus only on the "Don't do this" or "Because I said so" approach to discipline, you'll ultimately end up fighting with your children all the time. This will make them resent you, and out of spite or anger, they might reject the very values that are so important to you.

Instead, I recommend that you become a loving, caring role model for your children. For instance, Rini and I wanted *Shabbat* dinner to be a time of spirituality and fun for the family and an opportunity for us to communicate our beliefs and practices to our boys. We created an atmosphere that appealed to our sons while giving us the chance to perform *Shabbat* rituals. We invited other families to celebrate with us, encouraged our boys to join in the preparation of the *Shabbat* meal, sang songs at dinner (which usually encouraged the participants to relax), or read a passage from the Torah. Our boys grew up having a good time in our house on Friday night. When they became preteens and teenagers they "decided" to spend Friday nights with Rini and me, and they invited their friends to join us.

In the "sticker approach" to discipline, parents use a bribe to get their children to behave by setting up a reward system for individual behaviors. Parents say, "If you do well, I'll buy you a Barbie doll. If you're really good, I'll buy you a new outfit. And if you're super, I'll buy you a car when you're sixteen."

The sticker approach can be used successfully for some children with learning disabilities who need concrete reinforcement of good behavior, or for children four and younger. Most children ages five and older need to learn to respond without a monetary incentive when moms and dads say, "No, because I'm the parent."

I don't believe in democratic families. I believe in what I call the "benevolent dictator" approach to discipline. Don't ask your kids open-ended questions such as, "What time do you plan to go to bed?". . . "Are you thinking about joining the synagogue youth group?". . . "Do you want to go to Jewish camp this summer?" These kinds of questions get you into trouble by implying that your children have an equal vote in the family decision-making process. They don't!

It's better for you to offer a couple of realistic choices and let your children decide between them. Ask, "Are you going to go out for basketball or soccer this term?". . . "Are you planning to attend this month's *Shabbaton* or the one next month?". . . "Do you want to return to the Jewish Community Center day camp next summer, or would you like to try Jewish overnight camp?" As your children get older and show they can make competent decisions, you can give them a wider range of choices.

A very sensitive issue that needs to be addressed is what happens when your children violate or oppose a religious practice you expect them to follow. You want your children to say the blessing before eating, put money in a charity box, attend Hebrew School, and do the required homework. You don't want them to demonstrate disrespect to "Jewish standards" anymore than to "secular standards." (Math homework is no more important than Jewish History; French no more important than Hebrew!) When you establish rules you want your children to follow, you need to decide how you'll respond if they misbehave. It's best to evaluate and prioritize what is most important to you. You won't win all the time, so you need to choose your fights carefully. However, in all cases the punishment for breaking the rules should be communicated ahead of time.

When our boys were younger, if they didn't attend children's *Shabbat* services, Rini and I insisted they sit with one of us in the sanctuary. We expected them to be quiet, especially during the *Shemoneh Esra* (the silent devotion). They complained, "Why can't we play outside with our friends?" We told them that *Shabbat* morning is a time for praying, not playing. We also told them that if anyone broke this rule, he would spend *Shabbat* afternoon alone in his room and not be allowed to watch television Saturday night. Occasionally one of the boys would leave the sanctuary to "go to the bathroom." We knew he was playing with his friends, so when we arrived home, we'd send him directly to his room. Sound overly strict? I don't think so. To me, it's no different from cutting a school program. (In fact, I propose that the issue of prayer is of greater significance than, say, the "Holiday Band Concert" at the junior high school.)

I recognize that different families have different standards. It's an individual process for each family to decide which rules, customs, and traditions are important. However, I'm certain that you can add one or two or several Jewish practices to your family's routine if you wish to do so. Willingness and determination are all that's required. For one family, the decision to add more Jewishness may take the form of speaking more kindly to each other, even in the face of disagreement. For another family, the resolve may lead to visiting the local senior citizen home to read to residents. Some families may add Jewishness to their lives by turning Friday evening into an opportunity to have one dinner a week together. Others may increase their Jewish practices with the decision to end their dinners by saying the grace after meals.

Whatever Jewish standards or *mitzvot* you add to your family's life, I believe you should hold these Jewish standards to at least the same level as the standards of the secular world. You must be sure your kids understand your expectations, and you must stick to them. Remember, if your children lie to you, they lie—whether the untruth refers to smoking or drinking; failing to complete a homework assignment; sneaking out of a friend's home on *Shabbat* to go to a party; or not quite arriving at the Jewish youth group meeting they told you they were going to attend. It's your job to let your children know that lying or misbehaving about Jewish activities and responsibilities is just as serious as lying or misbehaving about secular ones.

Disciplining your children is a long, demanding process that requires determination and consistency. Truly, it's best to start from the moment your children are born, but it's never too late to begin.

THINGS TO CONSIDER

- Try to improve your definition of spousal and parental roles within your family.
- Consider the discipline style your parents used in raising you. If the techniques feel right to you, use similar ones with your own children. Otherwise, make modifications to fit the needs of you and your children.
- When you send your children to their bedrooms for punishment, do not permit them to use the telephone, watch television, listen to music, or play electronic games.
- Keep in mind that spouses don't have to agree on discipline techniques, but they should work together to set consistent behavior standards for their children.
- Don't compare your rules and standards to those of your friends, parents, or other family members.

ENDNOTES

1. Torah, *Genesis* 22:2.
2. Torah, *Genesis* 3:3.

Chapter 4
School Is Children's Work

Next to the home, school is the most important place where kids spend long periods of time. Five days a week, seven or more hours a day, school shapes their growth and development, and school has a lasting effect on their lives.

School is children's workplace. The work they do there is intense and important. In their workplace they have a boss and colleagues; they're expected to carry out assignments; they receive awards for good performance; they're punished for incompleteness and lateness. At the end of the work day, kids return to their families. For the Jewish child, education is more than a means of learning how to be a teacher, computer specialist, technician, surgeon, or nurse. Sure, the Jewish child's education emphasizes academic and/or vocational achievement; but, in addition, it should emphasize an adherence to Jewish ethical standards. A complete, fully rounded education for the Jewish child serves as an instrument for developing a concept of God and a tool for the performing of *mitzvot* (commandments). In other words, it cultivates not only the intellect, but the *neshama*—the soul.

THE PARENT'S ROLE

As a parent, you know it's important to take an interest in your child's school subjects, school activities, and extracurricular activities. You recognize the value of the parent–teacher organization. You keep apprised of your child's successes and failures, academic progress, interests, and social interactions.

Doesn't it make sense that as a Jewish parent you should be equally concerned and committed to your children's moral and ethical development? I believe the answer is "yes." I believe Jewish parents must monitor how their kids spend money, make use of time, care for possessions, treat their peers, react to the less fortunate, respond to the sick, pray to God, and carry out *mitzvot*.

Granted, such issues are much more difficult to evaluate and oversee, but parents should make a real effort.

One of your first responsibilities regarding your children's education is to decide between public school and Jewish day school. I believe a good Jewish day school offers the best framework for integrating secular education with Jewish education. At this point in the chapter I'll discuss Jewish day school; later I'll address the needs of Jewish students who attend public school.

A CASE FOR DAY SCHOOL

The most significant advantage of a day school is that Jewish values and principles and the Jewish calendar provide the foundation and rhythm. It's not just the fact that students in a day school learn about and celebrate Jewish holidays; it's that general academics and Jewish studies are integrated into one harmonious program.

Another major advantage is that most day schools have small classes, which allow teachers to meet the individual needs of each child. Students receive extra help in their subjects when they need it, and they are encouraged to move ahead when ready. The slower learner doesn't get lost between the cracks, and the swifter learner isn't held back. The overriding environment in a day school is nurturing and motivating, with an emphasis on enrichment and hands-on learning. These important elements are similar to those found in secular private schools. In addition, however, a good day school offers students an outstanding basis for the pursuit of further religious education and a meaningful Jewish life.

Rini and I made the decision to send our boys to a day school based on several factors. One is our firm belief that significant issues about life need to be introduced to children at specific ages.[1] We wanted our boys to discuss these issues as they relate to Jewish beliefs and Jewish values, and we wanted them to learn from Jewish teachers who would be role models for making these beliefs and values part of their everyday living.

In addition, Rini and I considered the statistics and discovered that children who attend day school are less likely as they go through the teen years to become involved with drugs, promiscuity, or other risk-taking behaviors. Moreover, most children who spend the elementary years in day school proceed to middle school and high school with the foundation they need to be academically successful, socially competent, and religiously committed. What more could Jewish parents want for their kids?

Our expectations have been realized. Our sons encountered teachers who encouraged problem-solving and independent thinking, imparted a love of reading and learning, and provided academic stimulation and emotional support. As a result, they acquired self-confidence and learned how to question, inquire, and think for themselves.

Equally significant, after leaving their day school, which went to grade six, our sons succeeded academically and socially in public school. Rini and I attribute their later successes in large part to the self-esteem and self-worth that the day school helped them develop during their earlier years. Their souls and spirituality were tended to in those early years, and as a result, they were adequately prepared to meet the challenges of the "real" world. For example, our oldest spent two years in Israel studying at a yeshiva while negotiating his military service and a prolonged hospital stay. Our middle son struggled with living away from home, studying at a yeshiva high school, and supporting himself financially. Our youngest addressed all the issues of being an observant Jew in a public school.

And even now that they're grown, when they

have free time (on a *Shabbat* afternoon, for example), they usually choose to curl up with a book, article, or essay.

There's also a purely practical reason for parents to consider a day school. In today's complicated society, a day school meets the needs of the many Jewish parents who are trying to balance two careers with children's schedules. When children receive secular and religious education in one school, parents are not burdened with the logistics of transporting them to afternoon Hebrew school sessions.

For kids, too, attending one comprehensive school is more pleasant and productive. I still remember how difficult it was for me when I was young to attend Hebrew school in the afternoons. After a day of public school, my classmates and I were already tired and wound up. We could not concentrate on our Hebrew classwork. Many children misbehaved as a result, and classes were disrupted. I survived, it's true, but I wanted to provide my three boys with something better.

Don't think I'm unaware of the arguments against day school. I've heard parents express the opinion that public school provides students with opportunities to mingle with classmates from other cultures and ethnicities. I've listened to the claim that many public schools offer excellent secular academics. I also recognize that cost is an issue. However, if you accept my premise that a well-rounded education for a Jewish child goes beyond academics, then you'll have to agree that the best school for a Jewish child is the one that encourages Jewish moral and ethical standards, fosters Jewish spiritual growth, and teaches Jewish behavior.

PUBLIC SCHOOL AND THE JEWISH CHILD

My recommendations aside, I know you may decide on public school for your children. If public school is your choice, I urge you to work extra hard to ensure that your kids receive a thorough education of Jewish studies and Hebrew language. Make a special effort to send your children to several weeks of intensive Jewish camp every summer. Be sure your children take part in a synagogue youth group and participate in *Shabbatonim* during the school year. Also, become actively involved in as many of your children's Jewish activities as possible, perhaps in the role of an adviser.

I suspect that those of you who opt for public school will send your children to afternoon religious school. (Such programs usually call for one or two sessions during the week and another on Sunday morning. Many religious schools incorporate the weekend session into a Shabbat morning activity on Saturday.)

If your children are enrolled in afternoon Hebrew school, be surveillant about the curriculum and faculty. Be sure the teachers are dedicated to, and capable of, creating excitement and motivation among the students. Be sure the teachers are good role models who introduce your children to the Judaism you want them to practice. Seek out membership on the committee or board that take charge of behind-the-scenes operations; become a homeroom parent; drive on special field trips; help plan holiday parties. In other words, do what you do for your child's public school.

Two important points: Don't approach afternoon Hebrew school as simply a step toward the bar or bat mitzvah. Encourage your children to treat afternoon Hebrew School as another significant activity in which they try their very best to excel. Hebrew School education must become an integral part of your child's overall exposure to Judaism (even if it never was for you). Spend a few minutes with your child after each class, and ask a few basic questions about the content. As your child learns in class, relate the learning to other daily activities. Discuss the relevance of lessons to your family's daily life. Visit the library together to check out books and videos that relate to the topics of study.

When your son plays soccer or basketball, you go to every game to cheer for the team. When your daughter gives a piano recital, you sit in the audience proudly.

Show the same interest in your child's study of Hebrew language, Jewish customs, and Jewish prayer. If you treat the learning that takes place at Hebrew school with interest, excitement, and care, chances are you'll influence your child to do the same. In other words, don't ever lose sight of the importance of this school and its role in creating a complete and competent Jewish soul.

PUBLIC SCHOOL CAN CAUSE CONFLICT

When children attend public school and afternoon Hebrew School, they may be exposed to mixed messages. Parents must be alert to the confusion and possible inner struggles that these mixed messages may cause. For example, public school presents academics as the path to professional accomplishments. Hebrew school is apt to rank academic and professional accomplishment as one of the tools we use to serve God in the practice of our faith. Public school might teach economics or delve into budget management, financial planning, or taxes; Hebrew School is more likely to teach that money is a blessing from God to be used to express His will and meet needs in society. Public school teaches students to treat each other fairly and kindly; Hebrew School teaches us to have compassion because we are all creations of God. Be aware of these kinds of subtle (and not-so-subtle) messages. Actively discuss them with your children. Most important, be a role model who encourages and enhances Jewish beliefs and practices.

A more obvious challenge to Jewish students in public school is the handling of the so-called "holiday seasons." I believe Jewish parents have an obligation to go to school to show others something about our rituals, customs, and beliefs. We should use these opportunities to underscore to the larger society that Chanukah is not a "Jewish Christmas"; or Passover a "Jewish Last Supper" or a "Jewish Easter." I remember how much I hated it when my mother came to my brothers' and my classrooms. I was embarrassed. I felt different. Well, Mom taught us that we *are* different and we should be proud of it!

Developing Good Work Habits

Whether children attend public school or day school, it's during the elementary years that they develop the good or bad work habits which will affect them during all their years of formal learning. This is also the time that they learn about being responsible for their actions. Make it clear to your children when they're young that you and their teachers will not accept assignments unless completed in full, neatly, and on time. If parents and teachers are lax, children will carry bad habits for the rest of their lives.

Homework can be a major conflict area between parents and kids. Take it from me, the key to a child's timely completion of homework is the parent's discipline program. Set guidelines by limiting television or other diversions and by establishing specific blocks of time when your children are to do their homework. Of course, you may offer some help and even go over your children's work, but don't sit down with them during homework sessions, and don't do the work for them. Sometimes kids with special needs require a parent's more direct assistance, which I'll discuss later in this chapter.

Your children should know that you're as concerned about Hebrew school work and grades as you are about public school work and grades. Otherwise, they'll learn that it's okay not to do their best in some educational situations. Moreover, they'll see that you don't consider their religious education to be as important as their secular education. Perhaps your parents didn't consider your religious education as important as your secular education and gave you that message. Even so, you have the power to make a change for the next generation.

I believe that any child who is capable should be expected to finish all secular and religious school homework and to achieve satisfactory or good grades in both schools. However, I caution parents against placing excessive pressure on a child with average or less than average ability. Familiarize yourself with your children's capabilities, strengths, and weaknesses; motivate them to do their best; accept their best and applaud it. However, I never like to see parents "pay" their children for each excellent grade on a report card. Encourage your kids to do their best work, and help them to view learning (and knowledge) as its own reward.

WHEN SPECIAL NEEDS EXIST

Keep in mind that children learn in different ways. Some children do better when lessons are presented visually; others learn better by hearing the material. Processing Jewish ideas, values, and behaviors that are different from those presented in public school sometimes can be perplexing for children. It's important for kids to have the right learning opportunities and for parents and teachers to be aware of how each child learns best.

All teachers should have knowledge of different learning strategies. Sometimes, however, it becomes the job of parents to make sure teachers are aware. For example, a child who has problems with fine motor skills might not be able to do an art project at Purim. Another child, who has processing challenges, might not remember the facts about Shavuot from one year to the next. Clearly, a child who has speech or language difficulties might not be able to recite prayers out loud. When teachers understand learning issues such as these, they often can help children achieve more success. Sometimes it's up to the parent to help the teacher understand.

For some kids, going to school is really difficult, even painfully difficult. Children who are hyperactive, have attention deficit problems, or suffer from depression, anxiety, or other emotional or mental conditions usually have trouble learning in school. For many children, such problems do not become apparent until the fourth, fifth, or sixth grade. At that point, teachers might begin to report that a child doesn't focus, can't seem to complete tasks, is easily distracted, doesn't retain material, won't buckle down and work hard, or some other similar complaint. If your child has any difficulties such as these, the exact problem needs to be identified and solutions need to be suggested by a trained professional. In the second section of the book, I discuss learning disabilities in greater detail.

For now, I'll conclude with this thought: As a parent, you're in a position to offer your child the encouragement, motivation, guidance, and discipline from which all future educational endeavors will develop. As you do so, always remember that a complete education means the development of the entire Jewish mind and soul.

THINGS TO CONSIDER

• Recognize the academic areas in which your

kids do their best work and help them become even more successful.

- Notice the areas in which your children need some assistance, and get them the help they need.
- Give serious consideration to Jewish day school.
- If your children are unwilling to succeed in school, set consequences for failure and then allow them to fail.
- Reach out to teachers to help your kids receive the best education possible.

ENDNOTE

1. Mishnah, *Pirkei Avot* (Ethics of the Fathers) 5:21.

Chapter 5
How about after School and Summers?

Wanting to experience what the world has to offer is a very Jewish concept.[1] I believe it's one aspect of the high value we Jews place on education, cultural enrichment, and physical fitness. I think it bears on the eagerness many Jewish parents feel about encouraging their kids to participate in after-school and summer activities.

One of the problems parents face is the almost staggering number of possibilities—team sports, art classes, music lessons, skating, dance, gymnastics, you name it. In most cities throughout the country there are teams, clubs, and classes to develop just about any interest or talent. While I, too, see the value in such pursuits, I also believe parents must be mindful of three prerequisites:

1. Avoid "overload" or "over-programming."
2. Help children experience the world within the context of Jewishness.
3. Make sure Jewish activities take precedence over other activities from the time kids are quite young.

Perhaps you paused at, "within the context of Jewishness"; maybe you flinched at, "take precedence over others." Did you shake your head, sigh in sadness? Whatever your reaction, it's a reflection of where you are on your personal Jewish Journey. I know from my own observation and experience that numbers 2 and 3 can be a real challenge, even cumbersome, especially at first. I'm asking only that you *think seriously* about the Jewish aspects of any undertaking before you lead your kids in its direction. I'm asking that you think and rethink as you raise your children, and I hope your thinking will be influenced by the conclusion that I've reached after years of Jewish Journeying. I believe that God created our physical and spiritual beings as one, that the body and the *neshama* (soul) are intertwined, and that parents should guide their children accordingly.

ACTIVITIES AND JEWISHNESS

If you want your kids to place top priority on their Jewish activities, promote them early on. Show your children that the most valuable opportunities for socializing, enjoyment, and personal development are the synagogue youth group, the Hebrew School, observing *Shabbat* and the holidays, and attending special Jewish events. (Needless to say, the year during which a child approaches the bar or bat mitzvah should be especially devoted to Jewish study and activity.)

To me, it's simple, again because of where my own Jewish Journey has taken me. Activities I rate the highest specifically embrace and promote Jewishness. I believe everything a Jew does should be aimed at enhancing his or her relationship with God and that parents should teach this to their children.

On the other end of my scale are activities that don't fit into the context of Jewishness (for example, anything that defiles *Shabbat*). For me and my family, such activities are unacceptable without question. I urge parents to think seriously about these kinds of issues and to impress their beliefs and values on their children. Just as with so many other things, laying the right foundation is very important. As you move along your path of

Jewish observance, seek your own comfort level and make adjustments accordingly. Once you start your Jewish Journey, you don't need to be afraid of changing and developing. As you feel the need to increase your level of observance, I promise you that you'll find the way to do it.

You may be thinking, "Won't my children miss out on opportunities? What if my kids want to play sports?" Well, I don't think there's really a conflict. Granted, if you want your kids to become Olympic stars, you might have some difficult decisions to make. Otherwise, I believe your kids can play soccer, or basketball, or take gymnastics or become good swimmers within the structure of your Jewish family commitments. Look for teams and classes which are in tune with your values, beliefs, and practices.

I won't leave this subject without a look at a particular challenge faced by many Jewish parents of junior- and senior-high students. I don't have to tell you how many public school activities are scheduled for Friday night and Saturday. It follows that this stage in kids' lives may reopen the need to wrestle with issues of Jewish observance. A couple I'm familiar with has a teenage boy who loves playing in the marching band. The other kids in the band are among the school's brightest and best, just the kinds of kids they want their son to associate with. After much thought and discussion, these parents decided to permit their son to play in the band on Friday nights during the football season. This is not the decision I would have made (nor would my sons have asked), but for this family, it was the "right" decision. This matter illustrates an important point to which I referred earlier. As each family proceeds on its Jewish Journey, struggles and challenges will surface, and they may have to ask themselves again and again, "What does our Judaism mean to us?" What's important, I believe, is taking the time to think and rethink in order to reach a meaningful decision. This is all part of taking the Jewish Journey.

SYNAGOGUE-BASED ACTIVITIES

I share the view espoused by many Jewish educators that parents should introduce their kids to synagogue life as soon as possible. I don't take credit for this idea! But it's important enough to deserve repeating. If your synagogue has a child-care facility, take your baby to services regularly as soon as the minimum age is reached. When you come to the synagogue together for *Shabbat* and for festivals, spend some together in the sanctuary until the need for a diaper change or fussiness requires your baby to be moved. Bring a small, quiet toy or two into services to lengthen the time your child can remain quietly in the sanctuary. As your child reaches toddler age, talk about the importance the synagogue holds in your life.

In addition to attending services, participate in programming aimed at families with small children. If you would like your synagogue to do more of such programming, find out how you and other parents of young kids can work together to create the programs you need. By the way, all programming doesn't have to be totally religious. It's also "Jewish programming" when the synagogue sponsors a Sunday softball game for parents and kids.

Avoid "Overload"

Talk to your kids about their interests and inclinations before helping them select activities. With so many activities to choose from, it's important to select carefully and to guard against over-programming. Start when your kids are in elementary school to guide them to one or two organized activities per week to enjoy in their after-school hours. More than that is too much.

Don't fall into traps such as making up for the chances *you* missed, keeping up with the neighbors, or wanting to give your children "everything." Don't use your children's activities for your own gratification. (You've seen parents who sit in the bleachers, boasting, "That's *my* kid. He's the star pitcher.") I urge you to value organized, after-school activities for what they are—a means for fun, exercise, developing skills, making friends, and learning how to interact with peers.

I don't suggest that kids should have unlimited idle time, but I strongly believe that organized activities should not fill every hour. Don't get me wrong. I'm not suggesting that it's good for kids to have unlimited time for watching television or pursuing "electronic entertainment." Quite to the contrary, I advise parents to limit such activity to an hour or less each day. What I *am* saying is that constructive relaxation, constructive "hanging out," is important to your child's development. Kids need some free time to play outside, ride a bike, sit down for a board game, read a book, or just daydream. What if they claim they're "bored"? I say, "Let them work it out." Learning how to manage boredom is one of life's important lessons.

If both you and your spouse work outside the home, after-school care is probably of utmost importance to you. Parents need to determine what after-school situation is best for each child. For self-reliant, responsible kids thirteen years and older, being at home without an adult might be okay. Personally, I prefer a latchkey situation, and I urge parents to find out if there's a viable program operated by their school, synagogue, or Jewish community center. Please don't forget that it can be unsafe to leave children at home alone for long hours. Moreover, many states have laws regulating at what age children may be left home alone.

DURING THE SUMMER

Make an effort to send your children to a Jewish camp for at least part of the summer. Encourage them to participate in activities at the Jewish community center or synagogue. But remember, the summer break is also meant to free you and your kids from organized activities. The summer season is probably the time most likely to afford opportunities for constructive relaxation.

The family's summer vacation is a challenge all its own. Of course you want to have fun with your kids, to enjoy "family bonding." Sometimes you're fortunate enough to travel, see sights, and make discoveries together. Keep in mind, however, that vacations usually involve special issues regarding parental discipline and Jewish commitment.

I believe "vacation parenting" is different from "daily parenting." For example, I strongly disapprove of the "bribery and sticker approach" to discipline in the everyday world, but I'm equally convinced that this approach has its place during family vacations. Go ahead and encourage your kids to behave by giving them candy bars; make a promise to buy a particular toy as a reward for especially polite conduct. But be sure your children understand what's going on. Tell them, in no uncertain terms, that things will "go back to normal" after the vacation. When you get home, be sure you revert immediately to a much sounder approach to discipline, as I've discussed in other chapters.

"48-Hour Phenomenon"

I tell vacationing families to take advantage of the "48–Hour Phenomenon." To do so requires tight, consistent parenting for the first two days of the vacation. If you're not rigidly surveillant for the first two days, I guarantee that by the third day, you'll all hate being together. So the moment you step into the airport and four-year-old Leah whines or runs off, you must immediately sit her down and isolate her—even if it's for only five minutes. (Only then may you resort to bribery!) Otherwise, I guarantee you that Leah's whining, running off, and other negative behaviors will escalate.

Vacations can be a time to strengthen your Jewish beliefs and practices. Remember, your children will watch how you handle yourselves to determine if you "practice what you preach." Seize every opportunity to show your children that your Jewish concerns and behavior are important to you. Make arrangements in advance to observe *Shabbat* and maintain *Kashruth*. If you say prayers daily at home, continue to do so. If you're accustomed to saying *berachot* (blessings) before and/ or after meals, continue to do so while you're away. Perhaps you and your family will consider adding another dimension to your Jewish observances by setting aside a few moments each day to recite the "Traveler's Prayer," which asks God to watch over you through completion of a safe trip.

Vacations aren't natural extensions of our daily lives, but with careful work in advance, they can be rewarding enhancements. Be prepared for the added tensions that come from being in close quarters without a break, and be ready to work harder to treat each other with care and respect. Sometimes you'll find it a particular challenge to remain patient and courteous to hotel employees and other service people you encounter, but you should try your best to do so, and you should expect your children to do the same. Treating others with courtesy is basic to Jewishness.

I remember when Rini's parents celebrated their fiftieth wedding anniversary by inviting us and their other grown children, along with all the grandchildren, to join them on a cruise. Rini and I planned for months. We arranged for kosher food and appropriate entertainment. We planned for the time we'd need to meet our religious obligations, such as prayer. We arranged for kosher wine so that we could participate in a *LaChayim* (toast), to the honorees. In addition, long before our departure, Rini and I talked to the others about the ways we observe Judaism, different from their ways. We wanted to do everything we could to assure patience, tolerance, and enjoyment. We were committed to practicing tolerance and cooperation without compromise. We showed respect for them and expected to be respected in return. All the planning paid off! It turned out to be a wonderful vacation for every member of the family.

I'll summarize with these thoughts: By balancing organized activities and leisure time, you can help your children make the best use of their after-school hours and summer breaks. If you've created a lifestyle for your children that's too highly structured and competitive, think about cutting back on organized activities. Select activities that will help your children enhance their Jewishness. Use vacations as an opportunity to strengthen the bonds of your Jewish family. Be prepared to amend your discipline techniques when you're vacationing, but be careful to stay in control.

THINGS TO CONSIDER

- Take every opportunity from the time your kids are very young to show them that you differentiate secular activities from Jewish activities.
- Encourage your kids to try different kinds of activities so they can find out which they like best.
- Attend your children's religious school programs.
- Make your kids finish activities they start, but don't be unreasonable. (For example, if your daughter joins a soccer team, she should be expected to complete the season. If your son

starts playing trumpet in music class, he should complete at least one semester.)

- Don't pressure your children to succeed in everything they do. Emphasize your wish that they enjoy themselves, keep Jewish values in mind, and do the very best they can at any activity they undertake.

ENDNOTE

1. Mishnah Torah, *Hilchot Dayot* 4:1, 14:15.

Chapter 6
Making & Keeping Friends

It's important to teach your kids to value friendship, not popularity. You need to show your children the meaning of sincere relationships and help them gain an understanding of human feelings, responses, and reactions. You should talk to them about such issues as approval, acceptance, rejection, compromise, and cooperation.

Having friends doesn't just happen. All kids go through a long developmental process as they learn the skills for making friends. At two or three years of age children undertake parallel play, and later they move into a peer group. For the most part, it's the peer group that strongly influences decisions on dressing, talking, and behaving.

Learning how to make friends, keep friends,

and be a friend comes from watching others, which is why parents need to be role models for their children. Your interactions with current friends—and your efforts to make new ones—will set standards for your children. If you're more concerned about the clothes people wear than how they act, your kids will learn that appearance is one of the most important criteria for selecting friends. Such a conclusion will underscore the incredible peer pressure that already puts so much emphasis on wearing the "right" clothes, participating in the "right" activities, and saying the "right" things. If, on the other hand, you seek friendships with those who share and practice your values of charity, prayer, and loving kindness, then your children will be apt to do the same.

Finding good people with whom to give and receive influence is a very Jewish concept. The Ramban writes that one's society/friends will have an impact on one's practices and values.[1] The Torah tells us about the "mixed multitude" who influenced the children of Israel in the desert. Recall, for example, those who complained about the lack of food. We, the children of Israel, had to disassociate ourselves from these complaints.[2]

Influence your kids as much as possible. Of course, when they're young, you'll select their playmates and determine when and how they play.

Until your children are nine or ten, it won't be difficult to maintain control over their friendships, but even as they grow older, and control becomes more difficult, you should never totally abdicate your authority. Continue to direct or influence your kids as they move from the "parallel-play stage" into the "peer group stage" and well beyond. When your kids reach their teen years, you will still have the power to influence their choices. Don't underestimate your power; rather, use it to the best advantage! Isn't it obvious that if you want Jewishness to be a high priority for your kids, you should steer them to the Jewish youth groups and the Jewish summer camps which believe in and practice Judaism according to your values and beliefs. Remember that important values such as kindness, spirituality, respect of tradition, and belief in the power of prayer do not happen in a vacuum. If you are committed to these values, you need to use the Jewish tools available to you to make them reality in your home.

INFLUENCE ISN'T INTERFERENCE

Be careful to distinguish between "influence" and "interference." Don't become so protective of your children that you strip them of the opportunity to work out their own relationships. Your children may be confronted with many difficult situations. Let them try to solve problems on their own. Many situations will not call for parental guidance. Choose carefully.

I look back on many times that our sons were invited to birthday parties on *Shabbat*. We encouraged them to take responsibility for explaining why they were unable to attend. A more difficult issue was the food served at parties. When they were faced with nonkosher food items, it was up to them to handle the situation. After being in a position to leave food uneaten or politely refuse to be served, sometimes they'd be teased. Sure, they'd come home feeling bad. Sure, these experiences were painful. However, as a result of working them out, they learned the social skills for negotiating the kinds of challenges that come up throughout life— especially a Jewish life.

One kind of situation that calls for parents to be especially careful is the meting out of discipline for misbehavior that occurs within a group. For example, your fifteen-year-old son has a group of friends you like very much. These are kids who care about each other's welfare, who take Judaism and scholarship seriously. Even so, one night when they go out together, your son returns almost an hour past his curfew. When you mete out discipline, be sure to focus on his individual behavior. Discipline him with complete "grounding" for a certain period of time. Don't cut him off from just the particular group of friends with whom he stayed out too late. The latter action detracts from a recognition of individual responsibility, and it could leave your son open to become involved with other, perhaps less desirable friends.

SOCIALIZING JEWISHLY

Socializing with other Jewish kids is important for your child from a young age. Seek opportunities for your child to get together with other Jewish kids at synagogue, at the Jewish community center, and at activities such as *Shabbatonim* sponsored by Jewish youth groups. From my experience as a youth leader, I know that out-of-town *Shabbatonim* are among the most valuable activities for preteens and teenagers. When young people go away together for a *Shabbaton*, they experience an adventure, enjoy a sense of independence, and share the richness of traditional Jewish observance with their peers. They also benefit from exposure to youth leaders who serve as Jewish role models.

These points are best summed up with this thought: To help your kids receive the support they need in meeting Jewish challenges, guide them to associations with peers who share and foster your Jewish values, beliefs, and practices.

Don't get me wrong. I'm not telling you that our Jewish kids shouldn't socialize with non-Jews. I'm the first one to recognize that our Jewish children will meet and develop friendships with kids from other religions and cultures. And sometimes Jewish kids who are very much committed to Judaism will develop friendships with other Jewish kids who aren't even affiliated with a synagogue, let alone making a Jewish Journey. What I tell Jewish parents is this: If you host non-Jewish kids or children less committed to Judaism than you, it's important to relax, offer a warm welcome, and proceed "as usual." For example, if you're accustomed to saying the blessings before and after a meal, do that. If on *Shabbat* you light candles and recite Kiddush, do that. Don't change your behavior. Do give your guests the opportunity to watch and, if they desire, the opportunity to discuss your rituals with you. Bring your kids into the process of showing their friends how you live a Jewish life in your home. Show your children tolerance and inclusiveness in the best sense of the term.

COOPERATION IS VITAL

As you raise your Jewish children, expect them to confront many serious issues and concepts which you'll be called upon to discuss with them. Among the most difficult concepts, I think, is differentiating "compromise" and "cooperation." Judaism teaches that compromise without offending calls for a difficult balance. I like to use specific examples to make the important distinction between compromise and cooperation. The following is one such example. It's based on a situation that demonstrates the importance of sticking to one's principles and integrity, but also striving for cooperation.

Let's say your nine-year-old daughter is invited to go to lunch with a friend whose mom has chosen a restaurant that doesn't meet your family's standards of *kashruth*. Explain to your daughter why she can't accept the invitation as is. Let her know you understand that it's important for her to get together with this friend, and ask her to help you think of ways to approach the other family. Perhaps the two girls can go for a picnic with their individual sack lunches. Perhaps you can invite your child's friend (with or without her mother) to have lunch at your house. Or, perhaps you could suggest that the girls go skating or to a movie rather than having lunch. By working with your daughter to solve the problem, you teach her a bigger lesson. Through careful cooperation, she can have a broad social life and also maintain your family's Jewish standards.

I suspect you're thinking something like this: "What if my daughter's friend and her mom don't understand? What if they're offended?" Unfortunately, I know that scenario all too well! Many Jews who approach their Judaism differently from the way I do have accused me of being "rigid," or "intolerant." If this should happen to you, state your position calmly. If necessary, point out that "tolerance is not a one-way thing." Don't let those who are less strict in their practices make *you* feel that it's up to you to change to accommodate *them!* Instead, help them appreciate your beliefs and behavior. Teach them how to be more cooperative. To say the least, it won't always be easy, but I'm convinced the end result of mutual respect is worth your effort. Moreover, remember that your responses to such situations will have an impact not only on your challengers, but on your children.

For Rini and me, ours has been a policy of tolerance and inclusiveness, and we've made that a guide for our sons. As a result, our sons are comfortable in practicing Judaism their way, even in the presence of Jews who practice Judaism differently.

Boy-Girl Relationships

The topic of socializing brings me to the sensitive issue of boy-girl relations. This is an issue that I've become increasingly concerned about as I've watched unhealthy changes occur. For example, I clearly recall that twenty years ago boys and girls in the six- or seven-year age range thought of each other as friends. Today, sadly, there are all too many instances where even at this young age, boys and girls interact as "boy friends" and "girl friends." Let's face it, twenty years ago our televisions and magazines were not filled with sexually provocative situations and photos; kids were not so much concerned about "coolness" or "sexiness." Sure, every generation struggles with similar issues, but I'm quite convinced that our so-called emancipated, enlightened age has encouraged far more emphasis on sexuality and male–female contact than young boys and girls should be exposed to.

Our Jewish youngsters need to play, not primp. Our Jewish preteens need to develop their individual talents, not go out on dates; they need to get in touch with their inner selves, not compete flirtatiously for each other's attention. In fact, at the expense of sounding "square," I submit that Jewish parents and educators must reconsider boundaries and standards different from those of society at large, and often they must come to alternative approaches based on Torah concepts. For example, I advocate school uniforms or dress codes and some separate classes for boys and girls. In addition, I urge parents to monitor and restrict provocative media in their homes. I'm fully aware of making suggestions that aren't embraced by today's society, and I know you might dismiss me as "out of touch." I don't think so. I've been a Jewish youth group advisor and a Jewish camp counselor. In these capacities, I work with pre-teen boys and girls and teenage boys and girls whose physical interactions are limited according to a strict interpretation of Torah concepts. Together, they sing, study, and learn about the cultural and religious aspects of Judaism. Together, they share feelings, work on hobbies, and undertake social action projects. All these activities they do together. Even so, they do not dance together or hold and touch each other. Nor do they become sexually intimate, because they understand that any such activity among unmarried males and females is contrary to their Judaism. I do not think it's merely coincidental that I haven't observed among these kids many problems with drinking, smoking, or taking drugs. I believe the lifting of the burden of "boy–girl stuff" enables them to feel freer, to be more relaxed, to have fun, to establish meaningful friendships. I believe other kids—including your kids—would benefit from Torah limitations in the same kinds of positive ways.

THINGS TO CONSIDER

- Make your home a pleasant place where kids choose to be.
- Show your young children how to play and have a good time by doing enjoyable activities with them.
- If your children are shy, let them make friends at a pace that's comfortable for them.
- When your kids get older, encourage them to use your home as a focal point for their projects and activities.
- Develop and maintain contact with the parents of your children's friends.

Endnotes

1. Mishnah Torah, *Hilchot Dayot* 6.
2. Torah, *Numbers* 11:4 (Rashi's commentary).

Chapter 7
Those Awful Four-Letter Words

I chose to include this chapter to make a statement about communication between parents and kids. I'm opposed to the use of "four-letter words," sarcasm, teasing, and unkind verbal stabs. It's the job of parents to become more aware of the subtle and not-so-subtle nuances of language and to make reasonable demands on their children's means of expression.

Kids hear four-letter words all the time in movies, on records, and increasingly on radio and television. They hear friends and older siblings expressing themselves with gutter phrases. They may even hear parents and teachers using them. It follows that they will want to use four-letter words, too. Well, it's normal for children to try out four-letter words now and then, but it's still not appropriate.

You need to decide where, when, and how much offensive language you'll tolerate from your children. You may believe such language should be forbidden entirely. It's more likely that you'll permit the use of offensive language when kids are with other kids, but not in front of adults. Perhaps you'll draw the line between "private" and "public." If so, use the subject of language to teach your children a few important subtleties about privacy: There's the privacy of their room, the privacy of their peer group, the privacy of the home, and so forth.

When kids use inappropriate language or in other ways express themselves inappropriately, parents should practice discipline—just as they would for bad grades, breaking a curfew, or refusing to give *tzedakah*. I know it can be easy to fall into the trap of responding, in kind, to children's mean, disrespectful, or offensive language. Don't let it happen!

There was a time when all three of our boys were disrespectful. It was a normal developmental stage. Nevertheless, we did not allow the language or the interchange to continue. In fact, that was a stage when our boys spent much time in their rooms as a result of their behavior.

When our boys were growing up, I made a point of teaching something to them each week at *Shabbat* lunch. In addition, during those formative years, we read and learned together from "Guard Your Tongue" by the Chofetz Chaim, the renowned nineteenth-century rabbi who dedicated his life to helping people sharpen their awareness of language. The Chofetz Chaim believed that God gave each of us two ears and one tongue for the purpose of serving Him, and gave us teeth and lips to help guard our tongues from speaking cruelly. This famous rabbi compared the destruction caused by a wicked tongue to death caused by a knife's stabbing, and he considered the former to be more painful and damaging. Further, he believed that the ultimate redemption of the Jewish people will be hastened if we are able to rectify the evil of cruel language and wicked tongues.[1] In "Guard Your Tongue" my sons and I found meaningful reflections about the use of language and about relationships between people. It took Rini and me a lot of work to create weekly learning opportunities for discussing this very sensitive subject. It was worth it! Our boys would tell us often how offended they were if they found themselves in the company of a disrespectful kid. In fact, they've come to Rini and me for advice in dealing with these kinds of issues.

STOPPING OFFENSIVE LANGUAGE

Many children begin to use four-letter words as early as age three. Sometimes they pick up expressions from parents who aren't careful with their own speech when the kids are in hearing distance. Clearly, a preschooler doesn't know what these four-letter words mean, so there's no reason for you to take offense. In fact, if you react forcefully to such words, your kids are likely to continue using them just to get your attention. Ignoring them will show your kids that the words have no special impact. Probably they'll stop using them. As children get older, however, you may need to take more active measures to stop offensive language. I recommend the technique of "Swearing for *Tzedakah*." Tell your children you'll respond to them in two different ways for use of offensive language. You'll send them to their rooms for a half hour, and you'll fine them a nickel, dime, or quarter for each verbal offense. It's important to avoid overreacting when your kids use four-letter words, but be prepared with consequences. Be matter-of-fact as you mete out pre-established discipline.

It's good to encourage your kids to express themselves by drawing, painting, or keeping a diary. And make sure they know they should always feel free to confide in you. Remember, however, that the constant use of angry language and the overuse of teasing and sarcasm sometimes represent an underlying problem. If you hear too much hostility from your kids, be alert to the possibility of troubles that may need the intervention of a professional counselor.

LANGUAGE IS A TOOL

Parents need to tell children that language is an important means of self-expression that can be used to help, or misused to hurt. They should give their kids examples of what it means to use language effectively.

Parents should remember to use language effectively themselves, especially when they want to influence, direct, and discipline their children. Let's face it, kids don't listen to long lectures. (After all, the attention span of younger children is only about fifteen seconds.) Often, however, they'll listen to us when we approach them out of context with concise dialogue. I call this the "10-Second Commercial" approach. For example, you're driving with your eight-year-old to Sunday school, and out of the blue you say, "Ya know, Mimi, sharing toys is a nice thing to do with friends." Or, you and your son are taking your bikes out to go for a ride together, and you point out, "Joel, you know that you're performing a *mitzvah* when you give to charity, even when you give only a *small* amount." Or you're cleaning the kitchen after dinner, and you mention, "You hurt my feelings this morning when you spoke to me with such impatience, Sarah." If your child responds, great. Follow the response with a question. Try to get some communication going between you. If it doesn't happen easily, let it go; try again another time.

A consideration of language wouldn't be complete without a look at a couple of phrases that much to my regret are becoming all but lost to kids. Simple expressions like "I'm sorry," "It was my fault," and "How can I make it better?" represent concepts that parents must practice themselves and teach to their children. In addition, Jewish kids have to learn from their parents that the concept of *chesed* (loving kindness) is more than the giving of money or other tangible things. I believe *chesed* is a state of mind and an act of faith, and I ask parents to be responsible for helping their kids understand it that way. Show your kids that the act of *chesed* requires the acceptance of responsibility in their relationship with friends and siblings. When your kids are as young as two, teach them it's wrong to use sarcasm or to tease or tattletale. Explain the importance of avoiding *Lashon Harah* (speaking badly about someone or spreading gossip). Even very young children can understand, when taught, that using sarcasm or spreading gossip can cause others to feel hurt or angry. In addition, make sure your kids learn early that a friend's confidences should not be shared with anyone else. Remind your children often that it's important to really listen to what others are trying to communicate to them. Teach them that listening is twice as important as talking, which is why God gave us two ears and only one mouth.[2]

I want to add a word of caution about communicating with your kids. There are certain phrases which have special meanings for every generation. When parents try to use such language, their kids usually consider them silly. Kids want us to be grown-ups and to talk like grown-ups, not to be their friends and talk like their friends. Parents shouldn't try to be "with it" when they communicate with their kids. Instead, they should use respectful language to their children and show them respect. They'll gain their children's respect in return.

Just as with so many other issues, when it comes to language and communication, parents should set standards for themselves and for their children. Let your children know what you consider appropriate or inappropriate, and be firm about your expectations.

THINGS TO CONSIDER

- Listen to the message behind four-letter words. Try to understand what motivates your child to use them. Encourage your kids to develop other means to express their feelings—both angry and joyful.
- When children are young, monitor the TV to avoid programs that use offensive language. As your children grow, set an example by avoiding books and movies that overuse offensive language.
- Use some of the study time you share with your teenagers to point out the precision and beauty of the language of the Torah and Jewish prayer.
- Teach your children alternative, inoffensive words to use when they have angry or hurt feelings to express.

ENDNOTES

1. Zelig Pliskin's introduction to *Guard Your Tongue* by the Chofetz Chaim.
2. Ibid.

Chapter 8
When Siblings Can't Get Along

Siblings fight. Their squabbles are a normal part of family life. Their occasional verbal barbs or mean-spirited interactions are equally normal. They clash over any number of issues: who will ride in the front seat of the car, who will sit next to Mom or Dad in synagogue, who will light the first Chanukah candle, whose turn it is to use the basketball net on the driveway . . . .

Many brother–sister conflicts include a strong dimension of competition, emulation, or vying for one-upmanship. Better known as "sibling rivalry," such conflicts can take many forms—some more serious than others— and often require judicious parental handling.

We're talking about complicated dynamics.

Even so, I believe four simple steps are extremely important for every family:

- Help your children *appropriately* express the resentment, dislike, or other negative feelings they occasionally feel toward each other. It's okay if your child says, "I don't want to be in the same room with Seth," or "I wish Rachel would go away and never come back." Your child might use even harsher, more graphic terms. Understandably, you may be prompted to reply, "Don't think like that." Well, sometimes your child *does* think like that! At such moments, it's up to you to acknowledge the feelings behind the words and to *gently* correct the specific form of expression. You might say to your child something like, "I know you don't want Rachel here. When you feel that way again, don't say mean things. Choose a nicer way to say it."
- Establish severe consequences for causing physical or verbal harm to one another or damaging one another's belongings.
- Provide ways for children to behave cooperatively sometimes, but don't be afraid of competition. I believe strongly that competition is okay as long as there's balance. Each child needs to win sometimes and lose sometimes. What's

really important is *how* the winning or losing happens.

- Structure ways that enable children to resolve conflicts on their own whenever possible.

Later in this chapter I'll discuss these steps in detail and show you ways that a Jewish lifestyle can help you adapt them to your family. First, let's take a moment to look at examples of sibling rivalry and parental response as charted in Jewish history.

SIBLING RIVALRY IS AGE-OLD

Perhaps the most famous situation of sibling rivalry occurs between the sons of Adam and Eve, who fight for attention and acknowledgement from God. Cain, the elder son, becomes angry because God likes his younger brother's sacrifice of sheep better than his own offering of the "fruit of the ground." Cain kills Abel. God punishes by making him a wanderer.[1]

Jacob's sons offer another example. Their experiences also pertain to the dilemma of parental favoritism. Jacob demonstrates his favoritism when he gives Joseph the many-colored coat. Joseph's brothers are resentful, fight among themselves, and finally throw Joseph into the pit.[2] The incident addresses many ramifications of parental favoritism.

Unresolved sibling conflicts can lead to "emotional death" and physical disaster. I've known families where brothers and sisters are equally hateful, and they suffer disastrous relationships. Sometimes responsibility for sibling conflict rests with the parents for not making an effort to help resolve problems (or for *always* resolving their problems!); sometimes siblings, themselves, don't try; sometimes it's a combination. I can hear you asking, "What can I do?" so I'll try to answer by looking at some of the teachings of Judaism. The rabbis tell us that every child should be taught according to his abilities.[3] I interpret the rabbis to mean the following: 1) Parents should be aware of each child's limitations and each child's intrinsic and developmental abilities; 2) Parents should treat each child as the separate individual he or she is; 3) Parents should again and again balance fairness while recognizing differences in their children's age, gender, talents, and abilities. There are two areas which call upon parents to treat siblings differently. One is the legality of inheritance as it pertains to the first-born male, since Jewish law specifies that the first-born male should receive a greater portion of the father's inheritance.[4] The other is the milestone of having reached the age of bar or bat mitzvah. Parents should consider a son or daughter to be legally responsible for carrying out *mitzvot* (command-ments) after the bar or bat mitzvah. For younger siblings, however, doing *mitzvot* is limited to the parents' obligation to educate and train them in these matters.

Many parents, in dealing with their kids of different ages, make two erroneous assumptions. They expect the older sibling to *always* be more reliable and mature. At the same time, they don't expect enough from the younger or youngest child in the family. I caution parents not to expect too much of their older children, nor too little of their younger ones. Instead, they should encourage each child to accept responsibilities that are age-appropriate. When our boys were younger, we seldom asked one to babysit for another, precisely for this reason.

While we're on the topic of siblings, I want to mention my regret about the lost art of listening to, learning from, and respecting an older sibling. Granted, an older sibling should earn a younger sibling's respect. Even so, I believe younger brothers/sisters should be encouraged to respect their older siblings and taught how to practice the respect that is due. A younger sibling has a great deal to gain by watching how an older brother/ sister talks, behaves, plays, works, prays, and relates to others. Needless to say, parents first must be sure that older sisters/brothers are acting in ways that they want younger siblings to emulate.

I'm aware of the delicate balance, and I urge each family to make an individual determination. Remember, there's a fine line between *encouraging* rather than *establishing* first-born (or older sibling) authority.

As our boys grew up, Jewish law often provided us the cues for increasing their responsibilities and privileges. Through Jewish law, we found the means to balance fairness while also allowing for differences in age and ability. For example, I taught each son to put on *tefillin* (phyllacteries) a few months before his thirteenth birthday. Each received his opportunity at the designated time.

The mere mention of "designated time" reminds me of the nightly bedtime, which was a major issue in our household. Our oldest required a longer period to achieve lights-out by his designated hour; our middle son went with the flow of evening activities more easily; our youngest would be okay if we'd succeeded with the older two. As our boys matured, we were careful to continue to adhere to different bedtimes based upon each son's age. It was no small challenge to balance family rules against the individual styles and the varying ages of each of our boys.

FEELINGS AREN'T ALWAYS EQUAL

When discussing sibling rivalry earlier in this chapter, I noted the favoritism Jacob showed his son Joseph. There are many other instances in the Torah of unequal feelings of affection by parents toward their children. For example, Rebekkah favored Jacob over Esau, his older twin brother, who was the favorite of their father, Isaac. Rebekkah helped Jacob receive the birthright from his father. This resulted in Jacob's having to leave home so an angry Esau wouldn't kill him.[5] When Jacob showed favoritism towards his youngest son, Joseph, he was, in fact, repeating the same cycle in his family system.

When it comes to parents and children, I think the concept of "fairness" is a frame of mind. I caution parents to see the issue in perspective, not to lose sleep over it. Recognize that it's not always possible to love and treat your children equally and fairly. My advice to you is two-fold.

Be aware that no matter how hard you try to be fair, you may not achieve your goal to your fullest satisfaction. Moreover, your children probably will not appreciate your efforts. I think you can consider yourself successful if your behavior towards your children helps to hold sibling conflicts to a minimum.

The issue of discipline–punishment serves as an example. To help maintain fairness in our family, Rini and I for many years have followed what we call the "Strike Three Policy." Our sons learned that after three "strikes" for doing something wrong, they'd be "out." (I should explain that "out" means nothing less than one full hour alone in your room.) As with most husbands and wives, Rini and I have different standards of behavior, different levels of patience, and different expectations of our sons. At the same time, our sons— being separate individuals—exhibit different behaviors that push our buttons. Therefore, toward one son, Rini or I might have zero tolerance for noise during *Shabbat* naps. Toward another son, she or I might have zero tolerance for sarcasm or for talk we consider judgmental. Nevertheless, by utilizing our policy, we have managed to be "fair" to our sons and to treat them "equally." (I wouldn't be at all surprised if they'd disagree!) We take comfort in the knowledge that we have deep love for all of our sons, and we have allowed ourselves the freedom to express our love differently to each.

At this point in our lives, our sons are young men. When they come home for visits, we still administer strikes for such transgressions as unnecessary disturbance on Shabbat, or talking back, or failure to complete chores. On such occasions, they may accuse us of being "unfair." Well, so be it, because we refuse to become hung up on the concept of fairness. Rather, we have come to an acceptance. We have come to accept the world and life as "fair" even though relationships are "unequal." We have reached the point where God provides the parameters for us. What might be seen as "unfair" or "unequal" is simply part of His definition of life. (I think it's a concept many of us don't understand until we have our own children.)

I think all parents and kids would be better off recognizing reality and acting accordingly. (Yes, kids are sometimes hurtful and mean; true, kids will sometimes tease each other.) As parents, we should be kind, loving, honest, and sensitive to our children's feelings and needs. However, we should not take it upon ourselves to try to "fix" the sad truths of life. My advice is that you use your parenting skills to help your children appreciate reality, that life is neither "fair" nor "equal," painful as that reality will sometimes be. Don't waste time on futile efforts to "make" life good, fair, or equal.

CONSISTENCY IS KEY

The concept of "fairness" often overlaps with "consistency." The latter is the more significant. To provide an example, I'll go back to the issue of varying bedtimes for children of different ages within a family.

Let's say the family establishes an eight o'clock bedtime for the youngest child and a nine o'clock bedtime for the three older children. If the parents become lax and permit the youngest child to stay up until nine, the older children will become angry that they are made to go to bed the same time as the youngest. They will probably be resentful and act out their resentment in some form of sibling conflict. In such situations, by being consistent in the enforcement of established rules based on age differences, parents probably will help reduce sibling conflicts.

I'll bring the discussion of fairness to a close with a few additional words of caution. Don't compare your children to each other (nor to yourself when you were growing up, nor to children from other families). Guard yourself against "taking sides" when your children fight. From the time my sons were young, I made it a rule never to talk to one of them about another, because doing so almost always sets up competition, favoritism, or both. However, the boys know that if they need to talk to me about their brothers, I will listen.

INESCAPABLE RESENTMENTS

Every family encounters situations in which siblings, themselves, will make comparisons, take sides, lash out verbally, or behave in other unpleasant, even hateful ways. That's why one of the three steps I mentioned earlier calls for parents to help children *appropriately* express the intense feelings of resentment they sometimes feel toward each other. Let's discuss in more detail what I mean by "appropriate" and make a distinction between "appropriate" and "normal." It's normal for a two-year-old child to bite, but it's not appropriate. It's normal for teenagers to be disrespectful, but it's not appropriate. It's normal for siblings to fight, but it's not appropriate. I suggest that parents designate a "Resolution Area" where problems can be faced and solved. (I'll go into detail later in this chapter.)

Given the nature of siblings, it's no surprise that the oldest usually resents the mere existence of a second child in the family. For some period of time, the firstborn was an only child and enjoyed every minute of it. To most firstborns, the new baby is an interloper who has stolen the parents' attention, and this is very upsetting. They don't understand that moms and dads don't love them any less. They know they aren't number one anymore and have to share their parents' time with an infant.

There are many subtle ways you can ease the "pain." If you plan a party in honor of the baby, a naming, or a ritual event such as a *brit milah* (ceremony of circumcision), try to bring older siblings into the celebration process. They might create decorations or placecards for the occasion or help extend invitations to family and friends. When the event takes place, ask one or two close friends or relatives to be especially attentive to the siblings.

It almost goes without saying that after you bring a new baby into your home, the other child(ren) will need to hear your expressions of love. Let your kids know that you care about them as much as ever, that you are still interested in their feelings and activities. Explain that you may not always come through, that new demands on your time and energy most likely will impede even your best intentions. This is another of the facts of life which older siblings have to learn. Feelings will be hurt. In fact, experiencing feelings of rejection at a time like this is an important experience. The feelings are normal, and dealing with them is a normal developmental task to be negotiated as part of life.

Siblings in a Jewish Home

I believe the concepts of love, care, and helping others are embodied in the philosophy of Judaism. If we understand them, we may be able to apply them to reducing some sibling conflicts. I refer to the commandments which put family, community, and religious commitment above individual needs.

I'm convinced children are better off when they learn early that belief in God and doing His commandments are more important than their own immediate gratifications. This certainly was true for my sons. From the time they were young, they saw our commitment to the synagogue, the Jewish Burial Society, a number of communal activities and to Jewish study; and they saw that sometimes these commitments had to take precedence over personal needs. This recognition, at an early age, taught them how to put others before themselves, and it helped them relate to each other considerately. Simply stated, it was a matter of taking the emphasis from the self to others—and, ultimately, to God. (Perhaps it need not be stated that parents must never neglect their own kids even to help the community. Remember, parents' first responsibility is to their own children.) Along similar lines, when parents encourage children to work together for the benefit of the entire family— to live with an emphasis on unity and cooperation—one of the positive results is a diminishment of their concerns about sibling rivalry. In the Jewish home, many situations lend themselves to sibling cooperation: working together to prepare a Rosh Hashanah dinner, creating costumes for Purim, readying the household for Passover, or just playing a board game together on *Shabbat* afternoon.

RESOLVING SIBLING CONFLICTS

No matter how smooth the sibling relationship, however, there always will be some amount of conflict. Ideally, the resolution of sibling conflicts should take place without parental involvement.

This gives children opportunities to learn the skills necessary for relating to peers and friends. By interacting with their siblings, children learn how to win, how to lose, and how to play with others in the real world.

When my sons were growing up, the ritual washing of the hands would start with the oldest and continue in birth order. When the younger boys became upset that they never "went first," I asked them to think about how we might solve the problem. Without any help from me, they came up with their own plan, deciding that the oldest boy would go first on Friday night; the middle son, first at *Shabbat* lunch; and the youngest son, first on special occasions.

It pleased me that they were able to think through their difficulty without any fights. Over the years, they used a similar alternating system to work out other conflicts, such as who would be first to put money in the *pushke* at the synagogue and how they would take turns playing with the Nintendo, using the computer, or riding "shotgun" in my car.

As I mentioned before, I advise parents to designate one place in the household as the "Resolution Area." This should be a neutral place, such as a basement playroom, not the family room, kitchen, or anyone's bedroom. In the neutral place, children can work out their problems, being mindful not to engage in any of the "Forbidden B" behaviors, which include biting, bleeding, bruising, or breaking (bones or property). In fact, you need to establish severe consequences for causing physical or emotional harm or damage to belongings. I recommend telling children they'll have to spend anywhere from half to a full day in their rooms if they break property or cause physical harm. In over twenty years of working with children, I've never, ever heard of one sibling seriously hurting another when they've entered the Resolution Area to try to solve their problems. However, you may need to monitor the situation without being seen. If you think dangerous behavior is about to occur, you should step in and send children to their own rooms. If children decide to have an argument outside the designated place, you must discipline both or all parties, regardless of who started the fight. Do not give any warnings, such as, "Go to the Resolution Area" or "Don't do that." If a fight starts, send children to their own rooms immediately.

Sending children to their rooms keeps you from becoming a referee or mediator. Many parents fear this method is unkind, too severe, and doesn't solve the problem of sibling battles. I speak from experience—both as a therapist and as a father—that in 99.9 percent of the cases, you can't tell which sibling started a conflict. It's best for you to remain uninvolved and objective—to let your children solve their problems by themselves. Children will work to avoid conflict once they learn that they're going to be in trouble no matter which sibling "started it."

How are children going to solve their problems if they're in their separate rooms? When it comes to getting their needs met, children are surprisingly resourceful! Since few kids like spending time alone in their room, they'll learn how to work out their problems so as to avoid it. I guarantee you it will take only two or three times before they'll have learned. Either they won't play together, or they'll negotiate terms before a conflict arises, or they'll compromise when conflict starts.

In sum, sibling conflict is a fundamental human interactive phenomenon—a fact of life—very similar to disagreements that occur when other human beings try to get along. You can't "resolve" the phenomenon totally. At best you can reduce or manage it. As I stated earlier in this chapter, Judaism acknowledges sibling rivalry and provides us with opportunities to diminish its tension on a daily basis. Your challenge is to recognize the problem when it exists and—utilizing the tools provided by Judaism—make efforts to achieve appropriateness and normalcy in spite of it.

THINGS TO CONSIDER

- Communicate to your children that you expect them to behave appropriately; you don't intend to reward them for it.
- Remind yourself often that sibling rivalry is normal, that your task is not to eliminate, but rather to manage it.
- Impress upon your children your hope that they will resolve their conflicts without your help whenever possible.
- Make use of dialogue on TV or in books and phrases in real conversation to help your children understand what you consider an appropriate way for people to talk to each other. Show them the difference between harsh, mean speech versus an expression of feelings that's polite, courteous, and kind.
- Give each child in your family certain age-appropriate responsibilities and make sure they're carried out.
- As you raise your children, be more concerned with consistency than fairness.

- Help your children learn how to interact, but let them know you *expect* them to behave appropriately, you don't intend to *reward* them for it.

ENDNOTES

1. Torah, *Genesis* chapter 4, 1–16.
2. Torah, *Genesis* chapter 37, 1–24.
3. Mishnah Torah, *Hilchot Talmud Torah* 1:6.
4. Torah, *Deuteronomy* 21:17; Choshen Mishpat 281:4.
5. Torah, *Genesis* chapter 27.

Chapter 9
Why Are Chores/*Mitzvot* Such a Chore?

Parents accuse children of selfishness and irresponsibility. Children grumble that parents make unfair demands. These are complaints I hear again and again in my practice. I heard the same complaints from my sons when they were growing up.

We solved the problem in our family, and many of my clients have solved the problem in theirs. The solution comes when parents impose certain obligations on their children—obligations which meet kids' personal needs and help meet the needs of the household. You might call them chores, jobs, or assignments. By whatever name, these are the obligations that become the "rituals of the secular world." Setting the table before meals, putting away toys before bedtime, holding family meetings, folding the laundry, suiting up for baseball practice, or joining together to celebrate birthdays are just a few examples. These kinds of simple rituals are extremely important to families, especially to kids.

All kids, from a young age, should be asked to carry out certain obligations, and parents should be clear about what they're asking. Parents will probably have to show their kids what to do the first couple of times. It's also important that they communicate to their kids, in advance, the consequences for failing to do what's expected of them. By fulfilling their obligations, children derive a sense of responsibility toward themselves and others. Their lives take on more order and discipline. They, themselves, become more disciplined.

In Judaism, we are fortunate to have a helpful guide of *mitzvot* (commandments) that are expected of us. As we translate these commandments into behaviors and rituals, they impose an even tighter order and discipline than the demands of the secular world. Often they make us stronger human beings. I believe, moreover, that the performance of *mitzvot* brings into our lives an element of spirituality and an understanding of the abstract concept of God. When Jewish parents teach their children how to perform *mitzvot* responsibly, they demonstrate an ongoing way to acknowledge the authority of God and express our gratitude to Him for his bounty. As they carry out *mitzvot,* children come closer to God. They experience a connection to the Divine by behaving in the ways that He expects of them. I must underscore the need for parents to *teach* children how to do *mitzvot.* Think about it. Children need to be taught to acknowledge and thank God, just as they need to be taught to mow the lawn, tidy up the kitchen, peel vegetables, make their beds, etc. For some Jewish parents, the ultimate goal is to have the family practice *mitzvot* together. They, too, start by imparting to their children a love for the process of fulfilling *mitzvot;* the appreciation for the actual act, the performance itself, comes later.

Children need to be introduced to *mitzvot* not as "good deeds," which are voluntary, but as requirements. Performing such simple *mitzvot* as washing the hands before eating, saying *Havdalah* (the ceremony separating *Shabbat* from the rest of the week), lighting candles on holidays, or reciting the *Shema* before bed—might be likened to looking both ways before you cross the street, using a fork and knife, or refraining from hitting another person. We're talking about expected, everyday behaviors. ("Buckle your seat belt! It's for your own safety.") You wouldn't do otherwise. As we repeat expected actions daily, our lives become more structured and manageable; fewer problems occur.

BELIEVING "SOME", DOING "SOME"

I'm not suggesting that you need to start by trying to carry out each of the 613 *mitzvot*—or even half of them! I'm asking only that you think seriously about the value of performing *mitzvot*, and that you begin with those that feel comfortable to you.

Indeed, a statement I made in the first chapter bears repeating here. I'm convinced that every Jewish person—at whatever point on his or her Jewish Journey—will benefit from "believing some and doing some." This certainly applies to carrying out *mitzvot*.

I've observed that performing *mitzvot* often makes people more precise, exact, and sincere. It's important to keep in mind that some *mitzvot* are commanded without giving human rationale (*chok*), some are logical (*mishpat*), and some are testimonies (*adoth*). By the time children reach bar or bat mitzvah (the rite of passage indicating they are growing into adulthood), they should understand about *mitzvot* and strive to carry out as many different ones as possible. It bears repeating that this knowledge does not come to kids accidentally. Parents need to teach them how to perform *mitzvot*, just as they teach them how to chew politely, how to share toys, how to wash and dress. Of course, it's best to start when kids are young, so that they learn as they grow that doing *mitzvot* is important. However, you can start the process with children of any age.

I started showing my three boys how to do *mitzvot* and chores when they were very young. In many cases the *mitzvot* and chores were performed at the same time. For example, before they went upstairs for the night, they made sure all their toys were put away. Then they washed their faces and brushed their teeth. Before jumping into bed, they recited the *Shema*. In the morning, they had to say a blessing before eating breakfast and then clean up the kitchen after the meal. Again, for each family, the *mitzvot* performed may vary. There are simple *mitzvot* that can be added to any family's daily routine without a great deal of difficulty. In my family, we say a blessing before we eat, put money into the *pushke* (charity box), study one sentence from the Torah each week, recite the *kiddush* before eating *Shabbat* dinner on Friday night, and avoid saying *Lashon Harah* (evil language) about someone.

Unfortunately, despite the declaration that

"God commanded" us, which is the ultimate commandment, children often don't perform *mitzvot*. Most likely this is because parents don't do them either. It's easier to watch television, fix up the house, or work out at the health club than to build a *sukkah*, study Torah, or visit the sick. The problem, I think, is that parents are sometimes too busy balancing family and work obligations to look at the total picture of life. Performing *mitzvot* has broad-reaching advantages for parents and children, such as helping provide structure to the family as you bring more Jewishness into your home; showing kids the unique, important relationship they can have with God; and, hopefully, motivating children to continue to fulfill His wishes. I promise you that your children will become better human beings for it! I know from personal and professional experience that performing *mitzvot* helps children become more polite, kind, and sensitive to others, and more responsive to meeting life's challenges. If you're having some hesitation, I plead with you to trust me; I've been there; I know it works.

One of the most important aspects of *mitzvot*, which parents must impart to their children, is that *mitzvot* are opportunities, not restrictions. Show them that following the mitzvah to observe *Shabbat* means they can spend special time with you, without the distractions of daily life. The family can sit down and have a leisurely home-cooked meal together, instead of eating on the run. Your kids can take a walk with you on *Shabbat* afternoon or sit with you at home and talk about what happened in their lives during the past week. Encourage your children to learn to read and speak a second language, Hebrew. Allow them to be more independent and attend a *Shabbaton* out of town. Praise them when they lead a service. It's important to show your children that these types of experiences are an enjoyable, enriching part of their lives. If you do this, your children will be more likely to embrace *mitzvot* than to shun them.

There's another point I urge you to keep in mind. You, as the parent, are the ultimate author-ity in the household. You have a unique opportu-nity to instill in your children commitment, dedi-cation, and love for the relationship they share with you. So, too, you must instill in them that you have expectations of them. Don't give your kids a "free meal ticket" to life. Why should they have maids called "mothers" and butlers called "fathers" cleaning up after them, doing their laundry, and giving them meals? I think it comes down, simply, to this: Often the reason chores/*mitzvot* become such a chore is that children do not have a clear understanding of what you and God expect of them. The code of Jewish law includes a delineation of tasks for appropriate ages. You can apply this information to the assignment of daily chores as well as the performance of *mitzvot*.

"4Bs" TO RESPONSIBILITY

I wouldn't be surprised if right now you're wondering, "Where should I begin?" You have a right to feel some trepidation, but I think I can help. Years ago I designed a guide for parents that I call the "4Bs" system. It shows how to make kids as young as six responsible for bedroom, bathroom, breakfast, and backpacks and how to handle discipline for failing to meet obligations satisfactorily. When I used the system with my own sons, I included, also, the *mitzvot* for which I expected them to take responsibility. The system worked for us, so I know it can work for you. Here's what you need to do:

Walk your children through all their chores, being specific about your expectations and showing them what you mean by a clean and neat bedroom, bathroom, and kitchen. Include in your explanation the *mitzvot* to be performed. At the same time, be sure your kids understand that failure to complete their chores/*mitzvot* will hold negative consequences, such as going to bed an hour early or spending an hour alone in their bedrooms. The amount of help your children will need in carrying out their chores/*mitzvot* will depend on their ages. For some time you should expect to help them say the proper prayers at the right time, complete clean-up projects, or fully equip their backpacks. However, your goal is to help them become self-sufficient, so that eventually they'll be able to do their chores and *mitzvot* without your help.

The obligations I have in mind should require only about 30 to 45 minutes. In the bedroom kids say the *Modeh Ani* (morning prayer), make their beds, and toss dirty clothes into the hamper or down the laundry chute. They also put clean clothes into the closet and dresser drawers, empty the wastepaper basket, and put toys or games in their proper places. In the bathroom they brush their teeth, bathe or shower, and comb their hair. (And they're expected to wipe toothpaste out of the sink, mop up water spills, and hang their towels up to dry.) Perhaps they will say the *Asher Yatzar,* the blessing after use of the bathroom.

At breakfast time, children prepare a simple meal and say the proper blessings before and after eating. (How difficult is it to pour cereal and milk into a bowl, or to toast two slices of bread?) Of course, for younger children, parents might have to make adjustments, such as putting milk into a small container so it won't spill. After eating, children say the proper "thank you" blessing, put their dishes in the dishwasher or sink, and put away unused food. Older children might also be expected to wash their own dishes. Finally, children are responsible for packing their own backpacks with books, homework, show-and-tell items, a lunch, pencils, permission slips, etc. (Get your "briefcase" ready for work, kids!)

Every morning before your children leave for school, one parent checks the bathroom, bedroom, and kitchen. It's easy to tell if kids have completed their chores, but impossible to determine if they've performed their *mitzvot*. Let me suggest two possibilities. You might post a chart for each child to mark off the finished *mitzvot*. Or you can ask your children if they've completed the *mitzvot* and trust they're giving you a truthful answer. I prefer the second option, because it's a way for children to build a conscience. They, and only they, will know if they've told the truth. Show your kids you trust them. Hopefully they will live up to your trust.

You need to be consistent and stick by the rules, or the system will fall apart. Even if every chore is completed (except one red Lego is left in the middle of the bedroom floor or only one *mitzvah* hasn't been performed), then your child has failed to complete the "4Bs" satisfactorily. When you're lenient and ignore one Lego or one *mitzvah*, I guarantee that your children will continue to test the limits. The next day you'll find two Legos on the floor; the day after that two Legos and a crayon. Every day the clutter will increase, and so will the numbers of forgotten *mitzvot.*

Kids need to learn to carry out their chores/*mitzvot* in the morning and at night without reminders from you. Did you just exclaim, "It's impossible!"? Believe me when I tell you it is possible. All of my sons accomplished these tasks, and from my practice I have taught other children who do the same, daily.

You'll be doing your children a favor by insisting they learn how to complete their chores/*mitzvot* satisfactorily or suffer the consequences. When they grow up and go to work, their bosses are not going to accept late, half-done projects. Make sure your kids learn how to follow rules early in their lives. Similarly, children must learn early that God doesn't like "half-done" *mitzvot.* God wants us to do exactly what He expects of us.

You can start working with your children when they're as young as two to help them develop the habit of being responsible. Young children can put away their own toys, do other small chores around the house, and perform appropriate *mitzvot*, such as saying the *Shema* before they go to bed. When you establish specific tasks for children and set consequences for failure to complete them, then chores/*mitzvot* won't be such a chore.

THINGS TO CONSIDER

- Make sure assigned chores are appropriate for your children's ages and they can accomplish them successfully.
- Do family chores/*mitzvot* together. Build a *sukkah*, clean out the cupboards for Passover, deliver food to the homebound elderly, rake leaves, sweep out the garage.
- For some chores, accept the best job your children can do even if it's not up to your standards.
- Be patient as your children develop the skills necessary to perform more complex chores.

Chapter 10
Mad, Sad, and Glad

Crying is a means that babies use to communicate. But in our culture, at quite a young age, boys and girls begin to express themselves differently. If we take a close look, we see male vs. female differences beginning at about the age of five or six.

Now, it couldn't be that little boys' tear ducts mysteriously dry up. We must assume that parents, teachers, and older siblings are imposing something that brings about a change. All it takes on the part of parents, I think, is for them to caution their boys that they'll look like "sissies" or "crybabies" or "mama's boys" if they don't stop crying. These are, after all, very derogatory labels.

So it is that boys of about five or six begin to translate their "sads" into "mads." I couldn't count how many times I've been in therapy sessions with young boys who are acting angry, uncooperative, and belligerent—while below the surface what they're really feeling is disappointed, fearful, or unhappy.

One young boy—missing his father, who wasn't able to see him for their usual Sunday visitation—felt sad, cheated, and abandoned. He wanted to curl up and cry. Instead, he started acting bratty to his sister and disrespectful to his mom. When he went to school the next day, he talked back to his teacher. Another little boy felt hurt and alone when his best pal, more interested in a new friend, didn't pay attention to him at the school lunch table. He sensed the tears about to fill his eyes, but he didn't give in to his emotion. So he tossed his sandwich at the child sitting across from him and started quite a ruckus.

I remember a few incidents when my own sons substituted "mads" for "sads." Years ago, I had a month that was especially filled with work and meetings, during which I was unable to be home for the boys. One of our sons became progressively moody and belligerent, and I knew that some of the problem was my absence coupled with

Rini's understandable inability to take the role of both parents.

When our son's "sads" about missing mommy and daddy were expressed in this particularly oppositional way, I saw what was really happening. Together, Rini and I talked to him about his hurt feelings. We used "soft moments" to listen. (Please look back to Chapter 1, "Parenting 101," for a full discussion of the "soft moments" concept.) Then, Rini and I made more of an effort to find times when I could be with each of the kids. And we also worked harder to make time for the two of us to be together.

What happens in later life to young boys who aren't permitted an opportunity to express their "sads"? Often they grow up to be bigger boys who express unhappiness (or anxiety, or disappointment) by being aggressive and abusive.

As for Little Girls

Similarly, something happens to little girls in about the same five-to-six age range. Parents and teachers caution them that even when they feel angry, it isn't "ladylike" to show it. They're told that "nice girls" don't allow themselves to be "aggressive."

What do they do instead? They learn to use "sads" to vent their "mads." When they feel themselves seething inside, they pout, cry, or whine rather than expressing their anger in a direct way.

Take the little girl who sat pouting in synagogue because she wasn't asked to join in singing *Adon Olam*, the final hymn in the service. Instead of expressing her disappointments through "mads," she sulked. Outwardly, she appeared to be upset and sad.

Like their boy counterparts, little girls who aren't permitted to express their anger also risk growing up without having learned how to express this emotion appropriately. If they're stifled when they're little girls, they'll get to be big "little girls" who continue to use "sads" to express their "mads."

Judaism teaches us that we will suffer the consequences if we don't express our feelings with directness and honesty. Look at Miriam. Instead of voicing her concerns directly to Moses and his wife, Tziporah, Miriam chose to express her feelings in a passive–aggressive way by gossiping behind their backs. As a result, Miriam was struck with a skin disease.[1] Consider Korach. He might have chosen other ways to challenge Moses than to humiliate him in front of the children of Israel. But humiliate him, he did, and afterwards he was punished.[2]

We Jews even have a festival, Purim, which on one level helps us come to grips with fears and anxieties that may be hidden below the surface of our consciousness. In celebrating Purim, we dress up in costume. Making a change in our outer appearance is a first step in helping us think about the fact that "things aren't always what they seem." We often dress up as characters which represent a threat to our safety and security—and this, too, provides an outlet for coping with some of our innermost anxieties. How comforting, how smart, that every year we have a means for expressing our fears, and we have such fun while we're doing it!

But, of course, the annual Purim Festival doesn't begin to answer Jewish kids' day-to-day emotional needs. It's of utmost importance that parents remain alert to signs that their kids are in need of outlets for expressing their feeings.

For one thing, parents must be aware of non-verbal signs. If you know your daughter is having a particular problem in school or at home, but she still appears to be cheery all the time—then you should be wary. Sometimes kids go around the house cheerfully, even in the face of serious problems, as a means of covering up their real feelings. It's up to parents to help them express and deal with their "mads" and "sads." Let your children know you care about how they feel; encourage them to talk to you; listen patiently and reflectively to what they have to say. Offer suggestions only when the time is right. And, of course, be a role model.

When is the time right? I recall once when our oldest son was acting out at school. We had no idea what was motivating his behavior. Patiently, we disciplined the belligerent behavior; and patiently, we waited for "soft moments" when we could encourage him to express his feelings. Remember, the peak of passion—the moment of dispute—is rarely the right time to talk. Parents need to be patient while also being diligent.

The need for patience, it seems to me, is another of the lessons of Judaism. For example, when we ask The Four Questions at our Passover Seder, we go through the symbolism of the four different children—the Wise Child, the Wicked Child, the Innocent Child, and the Child Unable to Inquire —in order to come to a composite of the many perspectives and behaviors that make up each individual child. Hence, we Jews are taught to be understanding and patient with others, even when others have a perspective that's different from our own.

"Glads" May Be Easier

While it's usually true that it's easiest for kids to express their "glads," this isn't always the case. Sometimes, kids are reluctant to express their happiness because other members of the family are having difficult times. Sometimes, they might have a nagging sense that they "don't deserve" to be happy. Sometimes, they're a bit afraid to acknowledge their happiness out of fear that it can't last. There are so many undercurrents, so many intricacies! Tough as it is, parents need to be alert to all sorts of emotions going on under the surface.

I have seen instances where kids in terribly troubled families—alcoholic families, for example—try to act perfect and pretend that their home lives are perfect. Why? Because they're making an attempt to present a "happy, good family." They want desperately to be seen as normal; they don't want anyone to suspect otherwise; they'll do almost anything to cover up the truth.

A significant happening in our Jewish history exemplifies how important it can be sometimes for people to hide their true feelings. Our patriarch, Abraham, ran off to welcome visitors following his

circumcision. He expressed the joy of having performed the mitzvah of *brit milah*, but at the same
time he covered up his intense physical pain.[3] I
can't emphasize enough how important it is for
children to learn when they're still young how to
recognize their feelings and express them in appropriate ways. This, indeed, is one of the wonderful advantages of a Jewish life! True, we have
many vehicles in our culture for expressing ourselves. We have sports, artistic endeavors, music-
making, writing. I submit, however, that the
Jewish faith offers the most valuable tools for
meaningful self-expression. Making noise on Purim
at the sound of Haman's name is a appropriate
way to express hatred and "mads." Dancing wildly
at a wedding is an "appropriate" way to express
"glads." Throwing dirt on a coffin and reciting
kaddish at the graveside are appropriate ways to
express "sads." Every single day, praying to the
Master of the Universe gives us the chance to talk
out our problems, to cry, and to plead.

I would be remiss if I didn't mention here another of the important dimensions of Judaism—
the built-in special occasions that provide a chance
to express ongoing joy. Every week we have
Shabbat; every season we have festivals. We dance,
we sing, we celebrate. In addition, I urge families
to create their very own special occasions. Simply

spending one-on-one time with each of your children is so important! You can bake challah together, create a menorah for Chanukah, take a walk, catch a movie, prepare a favorite snack.

Make sure that in these times together all of you have fun. Sure, seize these moments to learn what your kids are thinking and feeling. But, avoid using these times to lecture your children about performance in school or other serious issues. Above all, you must open up the lines of communication with your children and help them express their "mads," "sads," and "glads." This is a challenging task, because many adults have not learned how to express their own feelings. So, start with yourself, and then help your kids. Believe me, it's crucial for all of you.

THINGS TO CONSIDER

- Provide your children opportunities to express their feelings through drawing, painting, working in clay, dancing, or playing music.
- Use every chance you can to encourage your kids to talk to you about how they feel.
- Let your kids see how you express your mad, sad, or glad feelings.
- Go with your kids to see films in which char-

acters deal with emotional issues; afterwards, talk about what you've seen.

- Show your children that the Torah is filled with real human emotions and with examples that can help us deal appropriately with ours.

ENDNOTES

1. Numbers 12:1—Rashi.
2. Numbers 16:1—Rashi.
3. Torah, *Genesis* 18:1–3; *Rashi* 18:1.

Chapter 11
Generation to Generation

The preteen and early teenage years can be especially difficult for both parents and kids alike. Sometimes I wonder which generation has the tougher time.

Preteens experience physical and emotional changes, many having to do with hormonal development, those "raging hormones" we hear so much about. At this stage, too, there are often the beginnings of a change in the relationship between child and parent. One result is that many parents find it diffcult to guide or nurture, let alone stay in charge.

I think it's important for parents to be prepared with knowledge and a sense of humor: When kids are in the eleven-to-fourteen age range, be ready for rough going, especially when it's the first child in the family. I think the root of the trouble is that preteens want desperately to be grown up, but aren't quite ready to leave the comfort of childhood. They're torn between a wish to hang out with their peers after school, versus going home to mom for milk and cookies. They're torn between wanting to be responsible for their own choices and decisions, versus being stroked and reassured by their parents.

I'm convinced, however, that parents and their kids can survive—as long as parents are determined to be flexible and keep their sense of humor while also setting standards and imposing limits. Why? Because the setting of standards and the imposing of limits are the most important means of maintaining discipline. First, I think, parents should discuss with their kids all aspects of the behaviors they expect—from keeping curfews to abstaining from smoking and drinking; from giving *tzedakah,* to visiting the sick, to helping feed the hungry. Explain to your teen why you've set these rules. If you find it difficult to do the talking, ask a responsible adult who shares your views to do the talking for you. Or, provide your child with books that do the explaining.

How important are carefully selected peers at

this stage! As a parent, it's your job to make sure your preteen becomes and remains active with the synagogue youth group. In fact, I urge parents to propel their young teens toward assuming leadership positions. Moreover, parents need to encourage their kids at this stage to attend *Shabbatonim*, where they will be away from home while still remaining under the influence of strong Jewish role models.

I remember how beneficial it was in our sons' development for them to be active in the synagogue youth group and to go away on *Shabbatonim*. During the ages of twelve to eighteen, at least three times annually, they would participate in *Shabbatonim*, and at these enriching events they were influenced by other teenagers who shared the approach to Judaism that Rini and I were fostering in our home. Our boys invariably returned from *Shabbatonim* with exclamations of what a wonderful time they'd had. On our part, we were confident that the "wonderful time" included exactly the activities and influences we wanted them to be experiencing. Above all, we knew that the *Shabbatonim* were helping our boys to integrate the secular world into their Judaism.

It's up to you not only to set the standards, but to make sure your child maintains them. If you believe giving *tzedakah* is important, then you must ask and watch to see that your daughter regularly donates a part of her earnings or some of her allowance to a worthwhile cause. If you believe visiting the sick or helping the elderly are important acts, then you must require your son to carry out such activities on a regular basis. In fact, I think it's vital that you, also, carry out these kinds of acts regularly so that your child will observe your good example.

Similarly, if parents believe certain behaviors are not to be tolerated, they must set and maintain those standards as well. I think you can measure your success by this gauge: You've succeeded if your kid feels that he has "won" within the boundaries you've set. I recall a situation that serves as an example of what I'm talking about. When seventeen-year-old David was caught shoplifting, his parents took his car away and forbade him to drive. My feeling is that the parents should have taken away David's car for a finite period—say two weeks—and then, they should have allowed him to resume regular activity. This way, he would have experienced the same kinds of temptations again. If he were sincerely remorseful for his earlier transgression, if he'd truly learned a lesson, he would choose to behave differently in the future. On the other hand, if he reverted to shoplifting, it would be clear that he had not learned a lesson. In other words, parents have to be careful about overprotecting their teenagers. After all, when teenagers turn eighteen and go into the world as adults, they must be responsible for their own actions.

ADOLESCENCE: UPS & DOWNS

Parents should have clear expectations of their pre-teens and young teens and hold to their demands. For example, kids should be expected to do their chores at home and should be accountable for doing their classwork and homework. I believe parents should impose substantial consequences if kids participate in improper behavior or fail to complete assigned chores. For instance, parents might consider a restriction of telephone use or a "grounding" from social activities on Saturday night.

You'll recall that early in this chapter, I mentioned that parents of preteens will have to maintain a sense of humor. I know it's not always easy! For one thing, your mere existence is an embarrassment to your kids at this stage in their lives. The clothes you wear are unacceptable; your hair style is old-fashioned; you drive an uncool car. Sometimes their reactions to you will be totally exasperating! To successfully survive, you'll need to continue the good parenting skills you've worked hard to develop over the years. Listen to your children and be flexible when the situation calls for it. Above all, don't look upon your preteens and young teens as enemies.

Sometimes the ups and downs of adolescence will take the form of inconsistency in the way your kids relate to you. For example, you're a mom who's always had a good relationship with your twelve-year-old daughter. One day you go shopping together at the mall. At one of the stores you see a dress you think would be attractive on your daughter and show it to her. She responds negatively: "Mom, you're always telling me what I should buy. I hate that."

A few weeks later, the two of you go shopping again, and this time you don't say anything while your daughter looks over the racks in the store. Finally, she turns to you and accuses, "Mom, why do you even come with me if you're not going to help?" These kinds of encounters are what the relationships between parent and young teen are all about. One day it's "Let me do it myself." The next day it's "Please help."

THE BAR AND BAT MITZVAH

I believe the bar and bat mitzvah can ease the transition from childhood to adulthood, both for kids and for parents. However, I believe this positive result happens only in some, not in all, Jewish communities. Why do I make a distinction? Let me answer by sharing with you what I think the bar and bat mitzvah can mean to a young person and his or her family.

To me, the bar and bat mitzvah is one major part of a life phase, or life change, that occurs on the Jewish Journey. It's an extremely important turn in the road, which can and should become a milestone of development and growth. Two years before the bar and bat mitzvah, the parents can join the child in studying the Torah portion. Together, they can select additional *mitzvot* to perform in keeping with the Torah study. In the case of a male child, the father can start showing his son how to put on *Tefillin*.

On the bar and bat mitzvah day, the young person stands before the congregation, publicly affirming a commitment to uphold the principles of the Jewish faith and to accept responsibility as an adult within the community. At best, the occasion becomes more than a child's life cycle celebration—it becomes a family's life cycle opportunity, as, together, they explore and commit to the Jewish faith. In these ways, I think, the bar and bat mitzvah can serve to underscore a young person's long-lasting sprititual development. And, thus, a young person's struggles of "growing up" can become the entire family's challenge. It's so helpful for families facing kids' growing-up struggles if these are framed within the context of the Jewish faith. If parents and kids disagree over appropriate dress, decision-making, curfew, or family time vs. friend time, what a relief it is for everyone involved if they can be guided by the boundaries of *Shabbat, Kashruth,* or other *mitzvot.*

Unfortunately, I see that many, many parents do not think of the bar or bat mitzvah as I do. Instead, they consider it an "occasion," and they become more involved in planning the party than in isolating the *mitzvot.* I truly believe that everyone would benefit more from the bar and bat mitzvah if parents would limit the celebration and increase the prayer.

THINGS TO CONSIDER

- Carefully listen to your preteens and young teens. Hear the messages behind the behaviors.

- Reevaluate bedtimes, curfews, chores, allow-ances, and other rules as your kids mature.
- Encourage your kids to get involved in Jewish community projects, such as *Ma'ot Chittim,* Giving to the Poor at Passover; or *Shalach Manot,* Delivering "Goody Bags" to friends in observance of Purim.
- Know your kids' friends and keep in contact with their parents.
- Be patient of the emotional and physical ups & downs your kids are experiencing.

PART
TWO

Introduction

Before proceeding to Part 2 of this book, let me reflect on Part 1 and differentiate between the two. As you've seen, Part 1 concentrates on general issues of child-rearing such as meting out discipline, handling sibling rivalry, teaching kids how to be responsible with money, and helping children select and keep friends. In Part 1, I demonstrate many ways that Jewish belief and ritual provide a foundation for a meaningful life and a strong framework for raising emotionally healthy Jewish children. I also show that the parents' own Jewish Journey will have an important impact on their ability to successfully face challenges and solve problems which arise.

Now comes Part 2, in which I discuss issues

that are more specialized. These are issues that confront some, but not all, families, and often are chronic in nature (for example, discovering that a child has severe learning disabilities or coping with divorce). Some are issues that tend to create emotional turmoil and may cause one or another level of family transition (for example, a child's disabling accident . . . or the death of a young child's parent). In focusing on these and other specialized issues, I continue to demonstrate numerous ways that a Jewish family's belief in God and adherence to Jewish ritual can become important coping tools during difficult times. How much of a tool, I think, depends on any particular family's frame of reference regarding the Jewish Journey which the family is making. To me, there's an important self-fulfilling dimension to all of this: I believe that when the members of a family search within Judaism, they will find benefits; they will reap comfort and pleasure. For example, if a crisis occurs, a family which is familiar with praying to God for strength and guidance will be prepared to continue. As the members of this family approach their challenge through the medium of prayer, their faith will provide them the help they seek. Why? Because an individual's adherence to Judaism can help in facing any emotional needs, any circumstances, which arise. When times are good, the *neshama* (the Jewish soul) receives direction and harmony from Jewish belief and ritual. When times are difficult—even seemingly overwhelming—the same happens, as Jewish belief and ritual offer direction and harmony through comfort, support, and healing. So, it's from this framework that in the following chapters I discuss challenges and transitions that are non-standard in type or in seriousness. Continuing with my therapist's perspective, and keeping within a context of Jewishness, I suggest ways that Jewish families can respond to challenges and transitions.

I close the book with a chapter in which I discuss, in depth, the conditions and situations that signal the need to seek the help of a trained mediator, counselor, or therapist. Even before the final chapter, you'll notice many references to the important issue of when, and how, to seek professional guidance.

Chapter 1
Coping with Divorce

Everyone acknowledges that divorce causes disruption and pain to the entire family, but I don't think everyone fully understands the extent to which it can negatively affect children. Divorce can be so crippling to kids that the impact will be felt for generations to come. Why? Because once children live through a deterioration of their most important relationships, they may come to doubt their own ability to successfully handle intimacy and commitment. Such fear may go beyond love, marriage, and family—it may lead to difficulties in committing to a course of study or a career path.

I've counseled many couples whose families are disrupted by divorce, and I'm familiar with the psychological, social, and religious issues that accompany the transaction—before, during, and after. First, let me mention that over the years, in counseling families going through divorce, I've noticed that the ritual and structure of religion have provided them comfort and have boosted their confidence for embarking on future relationships and commitments. That said, I want to talk about a number of other issues, many of which also draw on my counseling experience.

One of the first matters I discuss with divorcing parents is their role in helping children confront and resolve the inevitable feelings of hurt, anxiety, and loss. This is of paramount importance. Without confrontation and resolution, there's a real risk that children will be emotionally and psychologically scarred forever. To be perfectly honest, I believe very few children can negotiate without professional help. That's why I discuss the issue more fully later, in the chapter devoted to when and how to seek professional help.

Breakdown Comes First

It's not unusual in divorce situations for the marriage to go through a breaking down period of one to two years prior to the parents' actual physical separation. I call the breaking down period the "emotional divorce." The parents' relationship is marred, the home is disrupted, fights and disagreements occur. One of the saddest aspects of this turmoil is that often the parents have become so involved in their own problems that they fail to notice the effects on their children. The children, however, respond all along, even if they keep their fear, anger, and upset hidden from their parents. In fact, I've seen many cases where children are brought in for counseling for "their problems" at this stage, while in reality it's the parents who need the counseling.

Once the divorce is finalized, it's not unexpected that the children, after a period of approximately two years, will "act out" feelings that were buried inside. For example, they might develop behavior or academic problems in school; demonstrate regressive behaviors, such as bed-wetting; express anger in inappropriate ways; or show signs of clinical depression, such as listlessness or constant sleeping. Of course, the form that such "acting out" behaviors might take will depend on the age of the children and the dynamics of the individual family. Some kids will work very hard to appear unaffected by what's happened to them; they may declare that "life is better now that the two of you aren't at each other's throats anymore." I understand that for some kids there *is* a real sense of relief. Nevertheless, it's a "relief" mixed with pain, uncertainty, and fear.

When very young children face a divorce situation, both parents should sit down with them to offer a simple explanation. "Mommy and Daddy are going to get a divorce; we're not going to live together anymore. This is not because of you!" It's very important to assure them that both of their parents will always love them very much and that each of you will work out ways to spend time with them. Older children, on the other hand, will probably ask questions that will be tough to answer. In my practice, I've noticed that within a two-year period following the dissolution of the marriage, most children become ready to discuss the divorce, what led to it, and how they feel about it. I must underscore the importance of recognizing when children are *ready* to talk and of then making the time to listen. Be prepared for children to ask difficult questions, such as, "Why did you marry Daddy in the first place?" "If you and Mommy were in love before, how did you stop loving each other?" You should respond in short, brief answers. Focus on the important point that people change and situations change over time—"Your dad and I have come to understand that we're not the right husband and wife for each other."

The Torah certainly has examples of changes that occur within people over time. One who comes to my mind is Joseph, whose feelings toward his brothers took a complete turn, resulting in very different behavior. Joseph felt and acted one way toward his brothers when he related his dream, but very differently when he asked their forgiveness after they were reunited.

No matter what you say about your divorce, never criticize or blame your children's other parent for what's happened. If you find you're not able to respond to your children objectively, I urge you to seek a mediator. A trained family counselor can be invaluable to guide parents at times like this. Remember, divorce is confusing to children on many levels. One important aspect for children's future mental health is for them to gain confidence that regardless of their parents' failure to "do it right," they, themselves, will be able to succeed. A professional counselor is trained to help bring sense back to confusion and doubt. I discuss the aspects of "bringing sense back to it all" more thoroughly in the final chapter of this book.

A JEWISH PERSPECTIVE ON DIVORCE

Jewish tradition calls on husbands and wives to do everything in their power to create strong families and keep them together. In an earlier chapter I discussed the importance of open communication between parents and children and the concept of *Shalom Bayit*, peace in the home. What if there's a breakdown in these sought-after goals? As with so many matters, prevention is the best cure, but the next best thing is early detection. Couples should make an effort to address any problem as soon as it's noticed. A trusted friend or family member or a rabbi can sometimes provide an objective outlook toward reaching a solution. It goes without saying, that sometimes it may be necessary to seek the help of a trained professional at this point.

The severing of the marriage tie is effected in Jewish law by a bill of divorcement, which is referred to as a *sepher keritut* in the Torah (Deuteronomy 24:3) and as a *get* in the Talmud. The bill of divorcement, a formal and judicial bill requiring sanction of a court, calls for stringent proceedings as befit a matter of extreme delicacy and seriousness. In fact, Jews should use a *Beth Din*, Jewish Court, to settle these disputes.[1] In cases of custody it is much more complicated, as Jewish texts indicate.[2]

CUSTODY AND VISITATION

I cannot emphasize strongly enough that parents, grandparents, lawyers, judges, and any other adults involved in custody and visitation issues must put aside their personal feelings to focus on the best interest of the children. Unfortunately, couples in divorce often have so much resentment and hostility that they lose sight of their children's needs.

Above all, visitations must be peaceful. It's helpful to set definite times for the non-custodial parent and children to be together. Be sure everyone knows ahead of time what to expect. Never let visitation rights become a tool for parents to use against each other. However, if fights do take place between the parents, the adults must be careful to keep the children completely uninvolved. If there are spousal fights, I believe it's important to say something like this to the kids, "Dad and I didn't get along while we were married, so it's not surprising that we're having trouble getting along now. Try not to let it upset you. It's our problem, not yours." In other words, protect kids from feeling caught in the middle; make sure the adults, not the children, are accountable.

Along these lines, I think parents need to reassure their kids often that they are not responsible for causing the divorce. They weren't responsible for the marriage, were they?! Sometimes, children actually try to keep their parents fighting once the divorce takes place. When divorced parents argue, the children still see them, on some level, involved with each other. Somehow, it seems as if there's still something of a "relationship." It's not unusual for children to hope that their parents will get back together again, and this "relationship" can tend to feed such an illusion. This is a terrible, stressful time for kids, and I believe that their lives must maintain a sense of continuity more than ever. How important for Jewish children is their religion at a time like this! Jewish rituals continue to offer a sense of continuity and security; the synagogue remains a strong, safe haven; the rabbi is still a wise adult who provides advice or comfort. I believe that for a child who feels personally in turmoil, such simple rituals as the lighting of *Shabbat* candles, attending Saturday morning services, and observing of Havdalah become more significant than ever. They provide a sense of structure and continuity. Indeed, saying the *Shema* each night is a significant daily reminder that God is there, even when life takes unexpected, painful turns. It follows, I think, that a child who feels "less alone" also will tend to feel "less at fault" for the event that changed life now and forever.

I think it's very important for parents to take turns with their kids in observing and celebrating Jewishly. It's neither fair nor wise for children to associate all Jewish holidays and festivals with one parent only. For example, children may spend Passover with their mother one year and with their father the next. Or, kids may attend a first Seder with one parent's family and a second Seder with the other. There are different ways to effect a taking of turns; it's up to individual parents to be sure it happens.

Sometimes divorced parents have distinctly different ideas about how they and their kids should carry out their Jewishness. Such differences can cause upset and confusion for children. If you happen to be the noncustodial parent in this type of situation, your influence, unfortunately, will be limited. The best you can do is to "plant the seeds" of your Jewish values and beliefs when your child is with you. As the noncustodial parent, you'll need to accept the fact that the greater influence on the child is bound to come from the custodial parent. But, never give up what you can and should do Jewishly. I recommend strongly that divorcing parents make a serious effort to work out such differences as one of the aspects of the legal settlement, before the divorce is finalized.

I want to share my experience with Seth, whose family came to me for counseling during the upheaval of divorce. Seth, who was quite upset by the divorce, found comfort and strength in establishing a new ritual for his life. He decided that he'd take responsibility for lighting *Shabbat* candles and praying the Friday night service himself. In spite of the fighting between his parents, in spite of the inconsistencies of two homes with different religious standards, he established his own structure. By doing this, he moved further on his personal Jewish journey. As challenges continued to present themselves, Seth sought and found solace in his faith and in the rituals surrounding that faith. I applaud Seth and I'm glad for him. Moreover, I include his story here to ask all divorcing parents to be mindful of their kids' emotional needs so that they might help their kids meet those needs through Judaism.

NEW PARENTAL ROLES

When parents divorce, both mom and dad should reevaluate their role from the new, single-parent perspective. Usually the dad is the non-custodial parent, and he needs to recognize how important it is to be more than "Weekend Daddy." He must keep in contact with his kids' secular and religious teachers, coaches, youth leaders, and friends' parents. The Jewish father who has his children for weekend visitation is responsible for instilling religious values too. He should attend *Shabbat* services with his kids. Sometimes, he should invite their friends to share Friday night dinner. If the non-custodial dad has visitation during Passover, he should be more concerned with maintaining an atmosphere appropriate to the holiday than "showing the kids a good time" by taking them on "spring break to Disney World." In other words, visitations are one imporant opportunity for him to be a Jewish role model. Remember, dad—fathering goes beyond fun and games.

The custodial parent, usually the mother, has specific responsibilities as well. When children experience strong negative feelings about their parents' divorce, they usually "dump" these feelings on the custodial parent. It's important that the custodial parent avoid accusing the ex-spouse for the children's negative feelings. For example, when kids come home to mom after visiting dad, they may exhibit behaviors that show mom they're upset. However, who can say for sure if a child didn't want to leave dad, doesn't want to come home to mom, or missed mom desperately? For that matter, a child might be upset for reasons that have nothing whatever to do with the parents—she might be in a blue mood, she might not want to do her homework to get ready for school on Monday. He might be having disagreements with friends at school causing apprehension about going back, or he might be coming down with a bug. One thing is for sure, mom: You must set boundaries as to what feelings and behaviors are acceptable in your family. You must continue to do your parenting in a firm, consistent way.

It's not unusual for the custodial parent (most likely the mom) to face disruption each time kids return from visitation. Don't let your kids push your buttons with such remarks as, "Dad's so much fun; why are you always so uptight?" Don't permit your kids to launch into complaints or laments. It's too much to expect of yourself to be able to maintain absolute objectivity. So, don't even try. When the kids return from visitation, greet them with a simple, objective statement, such as, "I hope your visit with dad was pleasant." Nothing more. Then, lose no time in suggesting that they get started on some activity that will take them to their own rooms, such as finishing homework or preparing clothes for the next day. The first hour of their return is the most critical, and isolation usually offers the best path toward a smooth adjustment.

I can sense your retort. After being separated from your kids for 48 or 72 hours, you feel they need to talk to you. Well, I think the "need" may be yours. You may feel a need to be reassured about their love for you; on some deep level, you may want to hear "bad stuff" about their dad or their "other family." Don't get pulled in! Maintain complete emotional distance from your children's "other family."

Later on in the evening offers a better time to regroup. Look ahead together. Open up a conversation about plans for the week. Tell them what you're thinking about making for dinner the following evening. Bring out the *tzedakah* box and remind them of their responsibility to keep up with the important *mitzvah* of giving to those less fortunate. Pray together. Say the *Shema*.

There's something else you can do. There are many good books that revolve around themes of Jewish kids coming to grips with real-life struggles and challenges. Go to a library or local book store for assistance in selecting books that your kids can read—or that you can read to younger children—which will be helpful to them. Discuss with your kids the characters, relationships, and situations which many thoughtful authors have chosen to write about.

DATING AGAIN AFTER DIVORCE

The issue of dating again after divorce is a very delicate one. Unfortunately, many divorced men and women tend to begin dating prematurely. I think it's a mistake to resume relationships before resolving individual "divorce pains"—those of the parents and those of the children.

When parents find themselves single again, I caution them to be extremely discreet. Most important, I think that new persons in their lives should not be introduced to their kids until the dating process has continued for at least six months. My logic is simple: Second relationships have less of a chance of succeeding than did first ones. Why introduce a new person into your children's life when the stability of the relationship is still very tentative? Your kids experienced a tremendous loss when you divorced, and they may be apt to attach themselves to your new friend. They might attach because they think it will please you, or they might attach because they yearn for "a new dad" or because they hope their father will start another family with "a new mom."

So, during the first six months, I discourage inviting your new friend over for a meal or going out with the kids to see a movie. Typically, dads who are single again are especially negative about my recommendation, because men are more likely than women to hurry into new relationships. Still, I say wait. Children who've lived through one failed relationship do not need to experience another. I'm not suggesting that you deprive yourself of a social life, merely that you keep your children out of it.

Let me summarize with this thought: Whether a divorce was finalized a month ago or several years ago, parents need to recognize the full impact of the experience and must be aware, alert, and ready to act. Very possibly, a trained professional will be the best resource for helping children (and parents, too) to resolve their hurt, make an important transition, and adjust to a new life.

THINGS TO CONSIDER

- Find out if your synagogue and/or Jewish community center offer activities aimed especially for children and single parents.
- If you're a single mom, seek opportunities for your children—especially sons—to interact with good Jewish role models who are also good male role models: Jewish youth advisers, Big Brothers, or other families' dads who share your values.
- Maintain social contact with other adults—single or married—because divorced parents must continue to "have a life," too.
- Develop a cordial relationship with your ex-spouse to promote a peaceful framework for children's visitation.
- If, after about a year, your children are still experiencing problems adjusting to the divorce, seek the professional help of a family therapist.
- Be aware that any future relationships you develop with persons of the opposite sex will have effects upon your children.

ENDNOTES

1. Gittin 88b; *Shulchan Aruch* Choshen Mishpat 26.
2. Eiruvin 82a, Ketubot 65b, *Shulchan Aruch* Even Ha-Ezer 82.

Chapter 2
Coping with Death

For a family with dependent children, the death of a parent is among the most difficult situations that can occur. This is particularly true when there are young children, for whom a parent's death can cause an overwhelming sense of grief and loss in addition to feelings of helplessness, fear, and guilt. Remember, kids sometimes believe themselves responsible when something terrible occurs.

When a parent dies, the surviving parent's role is particularly difficult, as he or she is confronted not only with new responsibilities and with fears about the future, but also with personal grief. It's a triple whammy and more, because very young children may become more dependent than ever on the surviving parent.

During upheaval such as this, the chances for making a successful transition will depend largely on the emotional health of the individuals in the family. As I have said already, I believe emotional health is grounded in a belief in God and an adherence to the rituals of Judaism. Further, I believe that both prove immeasurably valuable at times such as this.

Over the years, I've counseled numerous Jewish families confronted by just such a profoundly painful situation. I have observed, again and again, that families whose commitment to ritual is an integral part of their life find in their religion the comfort, support, and coping tools they need to meet the challenge. This was no surprise to me, and I trust it isn't to you. A well-defined commitment to Jewish practices and a strong belief in God often will be the most important factors in determining how well a family will manage.

If you and your young child (or children) are struggling with death, it's important for you to take one small step at a time. The very first thing to do is to help your child handle the immediate effects of the death before confronting the complicated long-term issues of the grieving process.

A surviving parent should expect to be called

upon to answer many difficult questions and to respond in some way to the unanswerable question, "Why has this terrible thing happened to us?" How you approach the subject of death depends on the ages of the children, of course; but remember, regardless of any reasoning you offer, it's equally important to acknowledge your children's pain and to express your own deep sadness. You can make a simple statement to a three-year-old, "Mommy's soul went to heaven." A child of ten or over, however, needs to be told something of more depth that relates to the universe—something theological. The particular theological references will, of course, depend on your own comfort level. Perhaps you'll say, "Daddy died, there's nothing any of us can do, and God wants us to go on." If the death followed a long, difficult illness, it might help to remind your child that "the terrible suffering is over now; Mommy (or Daddy) is at peace with God now; we can feel a sense of relief." For the family with a strong belief in God and Jewish law, I think it's important to point out to your kids that God's will is behind everything, good and bad. Life and death, wellness and illness, prosperity and poverty—no matter what happens to us, it is God's Will. Clear cut. That doesn't mean we won't be angry with Him or challenge Him when we face terrible times, but, ultimately, we must accept what befalls us; it's in His hands.

Judaism offers rituals that survivors can do. These are acts that help us mold the somewhat abstract concept of God's will into a reality. For example, we can observe *Shloshim*, thirty days of mourning. We can commit ourselves to study something Jewish in memory of the deceased or give *tzedakah* (charity) in honor of the loved one's memory.

For many kids confronted by profound grief, it's helpful to hear a reaffirmation of the surviving parent's belief in God. In fact, it's important for them to hear it often and unobtrusively. This is the time for the sort of declaration that I referred to in an earlier chapter as a "10-second commercial." Out of nowhere, you come up with a simple statement—"It's comforting to me to know that God will help us get through this." Once you make a comment of faith such as this, leave it to your child to talk about that comment, ask questions, or respond to what you've said. Allow for the opening; be prepared to talk further only if your child is ready. You may recall my mention earlier in this book of how important it is for children to know that their parents are believers. I talked then about the possibility of a parent's uncertainties and apprehensions actually interfering with the parent's efforts to make a child feel secure in a time of trouble. Everything else aside, the parent must continue to guide the child. This is yet another aspect of each individual's Jewish journey.

There's no doubt that kids react to death differently when a parent dies from a long, terrible illness rather than suddenly, in an accident or from a physical problem such as a stroke. For children who have not had the opportunity to "say goodbye," it will be especially important to present a simple explanation at first: "Daddy died because he had a heart attack." "Mommy died after she was hit by a car." Very soon after, sit down together to talk. Children often need to be helped to express their deep feelings of upset, disbelief, and anger. Judaism allows the time for this by calling for *Shiva* and *Shloshim* Days of Mourning, for example, during which a family restricts outside activities and concentrates on inside pain.

If possible, the surviving parent should initially sit down with each child individually. As tough as it may be, the surviving parent must try to speak minimally, but, rather, assume the important role of listener. Later, depending on the differences in the children's ages, it could be helpful to c ome together as a family. Remember, these are times for holding each other and for crying together. Sometimes it's helpful to bring out photos, draw pictures, and talk about the good times you shared.

Profound loss is apt to create uncertainty and turmoil, and you shouldn't be dismayed if part of that turmoil impacts temporarily on your faith. One of the most important lessons that my training and experience have taught me is how totally normal it is upon the untimely death of a loved one to experience temporary feelings of doubt, anger toward God, or another such lapse of faith. If this should happen to you, or to your kids, you must give yourselves permission to feel what you feel. Give yourselves time to "work it through."

I maintain that a family which is already well-defined in its Jewishness has the best possible chance to work through doubts and to reach a point of emotional survival. If you and your children have made a commitment to the path of Jewishness before you're faced with tragedy—if you are well along on your Jewish Journey—you may get stuck or even move backward, but you're going to be able to regain your footing. In fact, I think that moving forward, falling backward, and, perhaps, getting stuck here and there are all aspects of taking the spiritual path. With that thought in mind, let me say it's very troubling to me that many Jews—even some rabbis—haven't quite come to grips with the many-faceted impact that the death of a loved one will have on the survivors. I, for one, consider a temporary feeling of anger or other negative feelings toward God to be as "natural" a reaction as are anger, shock, disbelief, and sadness. Quite frankly, the survivors are entitled to it.

My interpretation is that Judaism acknowledges this, but also insists that we must continue our relationship with God. Even though we feel angry toward God, we must stand up and recite the *Kaddish*, the affirmation of His being and the recognition of His impact on our lives (i.e., His omnipresence). The Torah tells us this: Even when Moses felt troubled when God did not allow him to cross into the Promised Land, still Moses remained humble as he maintained his all-important relationship with God. I believe that the reaction of Moses teaches us that we are entitled to be upset with God. At the same time, Moses is the paradigm of how we humans should express our upset with Him: Ultimately, we must resolve it or come to peace with it.

"DOING WELL PHENOMENON"

There's another "natural reaction" that I encourage a surviving parent to be aware of. You might almost expect your children to hide their real feelings about their loss. They might pretend nothing has changed, or they might try to convince themselves—and others—that they don't really care. This is one aspect of what we professionals call the "Doing Well Phenomenon." Sometimes, the phenomenon emerges when a kid senses, almost intuitively, that the surviving parent is not able to offer emotional support. That child will put on a façade—carry on with life, go to school, play with friends, and act "perfectly normal." At some later point, however, this child will have to deal with buried, unresolved feelings.

I remember just such a situation, which I observed in a youngster I counseled. Daniel, a twelve-year-old approaching his Bar Mitzvah, was faced with the untimely death of his father. In spite of his deep sense of loss, he plunged ahead with his studies, explaining to his mother that he wanted "to do it for dad." Shortly after the ceremony, however, Daniel went through a noticeable decline. Fortunately, his mom was alert to her son's needs and sought the help of a counselor who supported Daniel through more extensive mourning, which he needed to complete before he could go on with his life.

One of the most valuable things for children to do when a parent dies is to look at photographs of happier times, to remember the good times you all shared before the painful death. It's important to talk about how much the deceased meant to you. Let me also mention that it's equally important to allow children to talk about ways that the deceased did not measure up, perhaps causing hurt in some way, even if unintentional. Some useful means for children to express themselves might be to write letters to the deceased parent; to visit the grave; or to speak individual, personal prayers. Often, these are ways for children to feel that they're continuing to communicate with the parent who has died.

Sometimes children will fantasize and express a hope that the parent will return. It's not unusual for kids to express a wish to die, too, in order to be reunited with the dead parent. You should listen to these feelings and express your understanding, but at the same time you must be firm in assuring your children that such a reunion is not possible at this time.

One of the important reasons for children to work through their feelings is to help avoid trouble in their significant future relationships. If children don't go through the grieving process, they may later "marry" the parent they had to give up so early in life; or, they may be afraid to commit themselves to marriage because they unconsciously fear that becoming attached to another person makes them vulnerable to loss. Other behaviors, which are even more self-destructive, could result later in life.

In our society, as you know, there are standard ways to try to deal with death. Among them are memorial services, funerals, and closing a business on the burial day to show respect for an owner or employee. For us as Jews, our religion provides the tools we need to cope with death, just as it provides us the tools to cope with life. Or, we can look at the matter in another way, which I certainly do. Judaism understands death as a part of life, and, moreover, recognizes what it is that survivors need to do as they cope with grief. Through some of these rituals, Judaism recognizes cycles that meet emotional needs:

> Sitting *Shiva*, the seven days of complete mourning during which one does not return to work or school. During *Shiva*, friends and relatives come by to show their respect for the dead and to bring comfort to the living. The *shiva* experience allows for the individual, family, and community to share in the pain and grief.

> Saying *Kaddish*, the prayer which proclaims God's absolute rule over His creation. This is an affirmative prayer which states that, ulti-

mately, we mortals are subject to the Divine Ruler of the Universe.

Observing *Yahrzeit*, the anniversary of the loved one's death. These are times to return to the synagogue and to proclaim again the unity and the will of God.

Saying *Yizkor*, the memorial prayer for the dead. Jewish tradition calls for the saying of *Yizkor* on Sukkoth, Passover, Shavuot, and Yom Kippur. While these are times to return to the synagogue to proclaim the unity and the will of God, these are also times to express a formal remembrance of the deceased.

I see these rituals as aspects of a larger process in which a surviving parent makes an effort to be an emotional anchor for the children. The surviving parent's success in being the anchor will depend, at least in part, on how much the family has become involved in living, believing, acting, and reacting Jewishly. It bears repeating, I think, that what the rituals of Judaism offer any family at its time of tragedy is largely a function of how far the family has progressed on its Jewish Journey.

Let's look more carefully at *shiva*, for example. The ritual challenges the survivors to accept the death and all of its ramifications. Rather than hiding in a dark room under a blanket, wallowing in misery, they must force themselves to receive company. They must not primp themselves, but still they must make themselves available to receive comfort from family and friends, who are performing the mitzvah of *Menacham Aval*, comforting the mourner.

DECISIONS ABOUT RITUAL

Among the responsibilities of the surviving parent is to guide children who have reached the age of bar or bat mitzvah in matters of Jewish ritual. Here again, the amount of challenge may depend on the extent of the family's commitment to Jewish practices prior to the death. How rigidly will the rules of *shiva* and *kaddish* be carried out? Will the children stay home from school during the entire *shiva* period? Will *shiva* be shortened to less than the full seven days? Will the children be expected to say *kaddish* three times daily, once daily, or once a week at *Shabbat* services? Will *kaddish* be continued for the full year? a month? or less?

I urge any parent in this situation to give each of the issues careful thought and to come to a decision within a Jewish context. It's up to the surviving parent to provide structure in order to help decide what to do and to make expectations known to children thirteen years and older. These kinds of challenges help parent and children to continue evaluating their Jewish Journey; additionally, these are the challenges that demonstrate the significance of the Journey in everyday life.

For a teenager or young adult, adherence to *halacha*, Jewish Law, is the most important and also the most needed upon a parent's death. I see this situation as an important opportunity to achieve a new plateau of religious meaning. I personally know a number of young people who committed to saying *kaddish* when a parent died and later continued to go to minyan regularly, be it one or two or several days a week. Having received comfort, they've made a decision to be a part of the community and to give back to others what they have received. To me, this is one of the great experiences of Jewish commitment.

It's interesting, and very sad, I think, that some skeptics call the ritual we've just discussed, a "crutch." They jeer at such activities as "dependency"; they talk about "lack of inner strength." How ironic that these nay-sayers have missed the very point! Sure, there's a dependency involved in carrying out Jewish law—a dependency on God.

But, we are frail human beings who need to be dependent, so what's wrong with that? Why fight a natural, human need? Why not recognize our deepest emotional needs and act accordingly? Think about it this way: We recognize that a healthy body may have a better chance to ward off illness than a weak body. So we give our kids multivitamins, feed them nutritious meals, and encourage them to get a sufficient amount of exercise and sleep. Why shouldn't their emotional health and strength require similar bolstering? Shouldn't we take measures to help our kids develop the emotional strength to face problems if and when they occur? The answer is, "We should, and we must!" Smart parents teach their kids how to thank God for His blessings and how to pray for continued blessings. If kids start praying to give thanks to God when life is good, they'll be able to pray to Him when life is not so good—when they seek guidance or when they feel the need to ask for a bit of additional strength and help.

I recently had occasion to make a comparison between two Jewish families in similar situations of profound grief, and I'll share them here to exemplify the points I've been making. The first family was confronted by the impending death of one daughter, a ten-year-old who had fought leukemia. When it became clear that medical treatment could not reverse the disease, the parents took leaves of absence from their jobs and brought their ill daughter home from the hospital. When I visited this family, I was saddened to find the that the parents had given up any interest in their own lives. Moreover, they were unable to respond to the secular or Jewish needs of their older children. They were spending hour after hour at the bedside, neither eating properly nor in any way taking care of themselves physically, emotionally, or spiritually. It was a truly terrible situation.

Quite a different approach was taken by another family. The mother, a relatively young woman, faced the impending death of her husband, who also had fought cancer for a long time. She, too, brought the patient home to be with the family in the last weeks of life. Even after her husband slipped into a semi-comatose state, she wanted his life to continue in a context of Jewishness. Each Friday the family prepared for *Shabbat* and observed together. Their focus was not on dying, but on living. Although they were aware that death was imminent, they carefully saw to it that the spiritual and emotional needs of the members of the family were being met. After their father died, the children told their mother that they felt close to their father's spirit while they carried out the Jewish rituals which always had been important to all of them. They received comfort during their father's slow death and observed him pass away peacefully. Observing *shiva* and saying *kaddish* followed naturally after his death.

I would be remiss if I didn't mention here that in many instances of serious illness, medical care in conjunction with faith and prayer lead to patient survival. I am convinced, you won't be surprised to hear, that getting well requires more than doctors and medicines alone. After all, even medical science admits that a patient's mental outlook impacts considerably on the process of getting well. In our synagogues, during services we read the names of congregants who are hospitalized, and we offer prayers for their recovery. I am convinced that when a Jew who is ill believes in the healing power of God and prays to Him for recovery, that patient increases the chances of recovery and survival.

THINGS TO CONSIDER

- Remember that the mind and the body both require nurturing for good health. Help your children develop faith in God and involvement with Jewish ritual so that their emotional strength will prepare them to face whatever loss and grief life may bring.

- If profound loss affects your children, be prepared to listen to their feelings of grief, anger, and denial. Don't be afraid to let your children know that you recognize that Jewish answers to death are sometimes confusing. At the same time, reaffirm your belief that Jewish answers to death are comforting. After you've listened to your children's innermost feelings and fears, help them to move on with life; let them understand that moving on with life is what God wants of them.

- Be alert to the "Doing Well Phenomenon" which is often observed in children after the death of a parent. Keep in mind that buried, unresolved feelings can cause many problems in later life.

- If your children experience profound loss or grief, give them "permission" to go through a temporary stage of anger toward God which, of course, may include a temporary lack of faith.

- Recognize that an adherence to Jewish Law in a difficult time offers an opportunity for your children (and for you) to achieve a new plateau in religious meaning.

Chapter 3
Kids with Special Needs

Special Needs. A term we hear often these days from educators and mental health professionals and from parents; a term that applies to so many different children. Sometimes kids fall into the special needs category due to internal factors, such as mental, educational, developmental, or physical disabilities. Sometimes their needs are special because of external problems; a home environment that's dysfunctional, for example—having to do, perhaps, with an alcoholic parent. One thing is certain: Where there's a child with special needs, there's a parent whose needs are special, too.

Disabilities come in many sizes and shapes, presenting minor and major challenges to everyone involved. If you're a parent of a child who has a disability, you must accept your child's limitations while still being positive about the possibilities that exist for accomplishment. As soon as you become aware of a disability, start communicating to your child a message that's both positive and realistic. It's so important for parents to face up to the problem that exists rather than to deny or minimize it. How damaging it is when a parent pretends that the child with a disability is capable of doing whatever any other kid is able to do. Parents must treat their child as normally as possible and be realistic in their optimism that their child can reach goals like any other kid; but they must also keep in mind that "normal" is a relative term.

Let me pause here to offer a very brief explanation of some conditions that are the most frequently seen disabilities:

Attention Deficit Disorder (ADD)   A persistent pattern of inattention which may manifest itself in academic, occupational, or social situations. Kids with ADD have difficulty organizing tasks and activities.[1]

Learning Disorder   A general category which diagnoses an "individual's achievement . . .

in reading, mathematics, or written expression . . . when it is substantially below that expected for age, schooling, and level of intelligence."[2]

Motor Skills Disorder   A "marked impairment in the development of motor coordination," a diagnosis made if "the difficulties are not due to a general medical condition."[3]

Adjustment Disorder   When there's a "development of a significant emotional or behavioral symptom" which is unresponsive to an "identifiable psychosocial stressor(s)."[4]

THE PARENT AS ADVOCATE

Parents can be instrumental in helping their child achieve success—in spite of a particular disability—within the framework of the child's limitations. It's up to parents to teach their child responsibility for behavior, and it's up to parents to seek out children whom their child can inteact with on different levels. Granted, a child with a disability may be awkward, painstakingly slow, or unable to perform certain tasks that other kids can do quite easily. That's why the parents of a kid with a disability need to encourage others—kids and adults—to be particularly patient and understanding in relating to their child.

There's another way that you, as a parent, can be an advocate for your child. While I believe you should seek expert guidance and advice, I urge you to be cautious. Don't accept the experts' assessments unconditionally. I have personally seen many kids whose parents have refused to write their children off—who have struck out against the so-called professional wisdom, who have fought for their kid, and who have won the battle. Nobody can fight for a kid the way a parent can!

As far as I can see, the biggest problem for children with special needs is in the area of developing social relationships. There are children with particular disabilities who can, with the right techniques (and, sometimes, with certain medications), be taught academic skills, homework skills, and chore skills. They can be shown specific ways to talk with another person or to share with another person. Even so, it's much more difficult to help them learn and utilize the subtleties and nuances required of successful personal interaction. This can become the most frustrating aspect of a parent's role. One bit of advice I offer is for you to seek out one or two others who have the same disability, or a similar disability, with whom your child can develop particular, special friendships. These would have the potential for becoming friendships beyond those developed with other kids; they would have the potential to offer your child especially comfortable, pleasurable interactions.

The National Jewish Council for the Disabled—*Yachad*—is one example of an organization that recognizes and responds to the needs of the Jewish disabled. Yachad means "together" in Hebrew, and this organization is aimed at helping Jewish individuals with disabilities enhance their social skills, identify with Judaism, and learn about and share Jewish customs. Chapters of Yachad exist throughout the U.S., and the organization continues to grow. If you live in a Jewish community that doesn't have a Yachad chapter, you might work with other parents to establish one in your community. [5]

EDUCATIONAL ISSUES

We're all familiar with the long-running debate about whether to be inclusive with kids who have disabilities or, instead, to educate them exclusively, by separating them into special classrooms. I believe children should be integrated into regular classrooms, if at all possible, and should also receive special educational services to help them with their specific problems.

What about Hebrew school and Sunday school? Well, you won't be surprised to hear that I believe every Jewish child has the right to a Jewish education. Our Hebrew schools and Sunday schools must provide for children with learning disabilities. To parents I say this: If your child has special learning needs, and if your congregation does not have a part-time teacher to help, you may have to get together with other parents to make it happen. Perhaps you'll have to go beyond your own congregation, to the Jewish Federation, for example. I truly believe it's your obligation to fight for these services.

I have made several suggestions here of how much work parents may have in raising a child with special needs. I'd be remiss if I didn't remind parents that they must meet their own needs as well. I know that raising a child with disabilities can sometimes be overwhelming, that the added responsibilities are sometimes crushing. The most important thing is to share the burden rather than to try to do it all yourself. You might form a team with other family members, such as grandparents and aunts and uncles. You might take turns with another family who also has a child with disabilities. In addition, you should reach out to teachers, group leaders, and counselors or other professionals.

No matter what it takes, you must maintain your own physical and mental health if you are to continue helping your child.

THINGS TO CONSIDER

- Network with as many good professionals as possible to develop a cooperative effort in helping your child meet his or her particular challenges.
- Allow your child to have as much responsibility as possible in making choices and living life.
- Don't try to shield your child from every struggle and pain connected to dealing with personal limitations.
- For your benefit as well as your child's, connect with other Jewish families whose kids have similar problems.
- Be your child's best advocate regarding school and religious school.
- Be patient and understanding of your child, especially in the social arena.

ENDNOTES

1. *DSM-IV*, Published by the American Psychiatric Association, Washington, D.C., 1994, pp. 78–79.
2. Ibid. p. 46.
3. Ibid. p. 53.
4. Ibid. p. 623.
5. Yachad can be reached at 333 Seventh Ave., New York, N.Y. 10001; Telephone: (212) 613-8229; FAX: (212) 564-9058.

Chapter 4

When and How to Choose a Therapist

Most parents feel comfortable responding to their kids' minor medical needs. Scrapes, cuts, and bruises require the first-aid kit in the kitchen; sore throats and runny noses call for chicken soup and over-the-counter drugs. But if the skin around the cut becomes red and hot, if a sore throat lasts for a week, if a lingering cough impedes sleep, then it's time to seek the attention of a medical professional. Length of time and severity of ailment dictate the course of action.

So, too, with emotional problems. If a parent observes a serious problem—such as continued temper tantrums, a drop in grades, or self-hate—

and if that serious problem lasts a long time, it's wise to seek the help of a professional. Let me emphasize that in using the term "professional," I mean someone trained to assist in mediating and/or exploring solutions. Now, I suspect you're wondering, "What's a 'long time'?" To answer that, I advise you to trust your intuition. Try to solve problems on your own; wait a few weeks to see if things turn around. If you feel that the problem isn't turning around or that it's going from bad to worse, don't wait six months, or a year, to take a step.

Selecting the right professional is just as important as knowing when to begin the search. There are a number of good ways to start looking. I don't have to tell you that going to the yellow pages isn't one of them! You might ask a relative or intimate friend to make a referral. A school counselor, teacher, or member of the clergy may be able to steer you. First, try to define for yourself what you think may be the cause of the problem. Is the problem rooted in a severe learning disability? Is the main issue sibling rivalry? Do you and your spouse have problems that affect the kids? Do you feel inadequate in the parental role? Do you suspect substance abuse or a severe mental health issue? Perhaps you sense that something's wrong, but have no clue about the actual cause.

One way to define the problem is to ask yourself two questions:

> With the help of a therapist, what do I hope to accomplish?

> With the help of a therapist, what would I like to change?

Your efforts to find the right therapist will be that much easier the more you're able to pinpoint what needs to be done. However—and I can't emphasize this enough—if you're just plain stuck, don't turn off to the importance of finding a professional. When you're stuck, it could be the time you need help the most.

As I'm sure you know, there are several different types of professionals who do therapy and counseling—psychologists, psychiatrists, social workers, and clergy. It would be helpful for you to understand how they differ, so I'll offer a brief overview here, even though I'm aware that my overview might be a bit biased because I'm a social worker and partial to this group's approach. My perspective follows:

Psychiatrists are physicians with additional training in mental health. They can prescribe medication to manage a wide range of psychiatric symptoms. Psychiatrists usually look at an individual's problems from a medical model. Most psychiatrists provide psychotherapy and counseling in addition to pharmacological interventions.

Psychologists provide psychotherapy and counseling to individuals, groups, couples, and families. They are trained in the administration and interpretation of psychological measures for assessing intelligence, personality traits, behavioral problems, and psychopathology. Psychologists also are trained to do psychotherapy or counseling, often with an area of specialization. Typically, they view psychological problems from an individual or family perspective.

Social workers and counselors are committed to therapy aimed at providing therapeutic intervention. They help individuals and families express their feelings and problems. They help in sorting out and coming to grips with difficulties. They work with schools, physicians, social agencies, and other professionals to solve problems. They use a systems approach which goes beyond the individual. In other words, they look at kids within the totality of their environments—such as the family, the school, friends, or extra-curricular activities.

Members of the clergy often do counseling as a part of their congregational work. Of course, their level of training varies. Individual members of the clergy, depending on their training and licensure, may be permitted to do therapy. Sometimes parents will start by taking their child to see their spiritual leader and then pursue therapy with a professional outside the religious setting.

There are two main points I'd like to make to parents who are considering professional help: First, remember that children's problems (including issues involving children versus parents) should be handled only by a professional with specific training and experience in working with kids and families. Second, be sure you're committed to making a change and willing to take the time necessary to bring it about. In other words, there are many problems that cannot be solved in five or six sessions, or even in several months. There are some deep-seated issues that lead to extremely problematic behaviors (behaviors such as "soiling" or broad defiance), and these require ongoing counseling/therapy.

This brings me to several related issues of the utmost delicacy:

1. Please keep in mind that therapy, like life, often ebbs and flows because it's progressive and regressive. That is precisely why it's critical to have ongoing dialogue between the family and the professional.
2. Sometimes a child who's in therapy develops negative feelings toward the therapist. Such temporary negativity is not necessarily an indicator that the therapy is unsuccessful. In fact, a negative child–therapist relationship can be part of a painful struggle that a child needs to act out before it's possible to work toward change.
3. A Jewish family may wonder about the wisdom of seeking a therapist who is Jewish also. Perhaps a Jewish family may wonder about the wisdom of seeking a therapist whose ways of practicing Judaism are rather closely allied to their own. Sure, there are sensitive issues. However, I'll tell you, without qualification, I believe a competent, well-trained professional will be able to help a family regardless of social, economic, and religious similarities or differences.

Don't get me wrong. I absolutely do recognize the initial "comfort level" of talking to a professional who understands "where you're coming from." Sometimes there are very specific issues that a professional of similar religious, economic, or social background will be able to empathize with, and that will probably mean the therapy will proceed at a quicker pace. I think these kinds of "empathy issues" require more exploration. Until such time as actual studies are conducted, my advice to parents is that they concern themselves with the therapist's training, experience, and reputation. After that, they'll have to trust their own intuition and feel out their comfort level with the therapist they've chosen. I suggest that parents give therapy four, five, or six sessions. If they do not feel comfortable, they should not be reluctant to make a change. "Let's get a second opinion!"

I'd be remiss if I didn't mention several other related matters:

1. Definitions about training and licensure vary from state to state. So, too, do expectations. Therefore, I urge parents to do their research carefully and then to go into therapy with a positive attitude.
2. Check out the financial aspects of going into therapy before you do it. Clarify the costs and

determine whether you have insurance policies that may be tapped to help you cover the costs.

3. Once you've entered into therapy, it's important to evaluate the successes and failures of the sessions. Parents should do these evaluations with the professional. Some problems require more time and attention. Like life, therapy can be a rocky road—progressive and regressive and necessitating ongoing communication. It's the ongoing dialogue between family and professional that is the critical element—even if, as I mentioned earlier in this chapter, sometimes the child may develop negative feelings toward the professional.

I will be the first person to admit that therapy sometimes can be very difficult. At the same time, I am the first to say that seeking and undergoing therapy can be one of the most important family decisions parents make toward assuring ongoing mental health for themselves and their children.

Epilogue

As my book comes to an end, I recognize that for you, my reader, the work may just be starting. Let me phrase my thought another way: I sincerely hope I have inspired you to think deeply about yourself, your spouse, and your children and to proceed on your own Jewish Journey. Truly, I understand that the going might be tough, but I also know that the outcome will be well worth the effort. Moreover, I have every confidence that with the help of God you will succeed. I wish you the best.

Index

About the Author

Allan M. Gonsher, LCSW, ACSW, is the founder and President of Kids, Inc., a counseling agency for families and children up to age thirteen. He has a Master's Degree in Social Work from Columbia University. He is active in the Omaha Jewish community and has been instrumental in developing educational experiences for children, teenagers, and adults. Allan combined his love of children and Judaism to write *An Allowance Is Not a Bribe: and Other Helpful Hints for Raising Responsible Jewish Children.* He shares his personal experiences with readers to show them how loving discipline can be combined with the practices of Judaism. Allan and his wife, Rini, used many of the techniques in this book to raise their three sons.